What readers are saying about

THE PERSONAL
TRAVEL SAFETY MANUAL:

"The environment for international travel has changed. Preparation, security planning, and sound safety precautions are now vital considerations. The very practical advice in this book will enhance your safety awareness, improve your personal security, and probably raise your business effectiveness."

— Stanley D. Loar, CEO, Woodruff-Sawyer &Co., an Assurex Global Partner for International Insurance and Risk Management

"I wouldn't dream of planning a trip without a careful study of what this excellent little book contains, and I would then include it in my luggage."

— Robert Pepper, former Deputy Director and Chief of Staff, British Army Intelligence Corps; head of international security at Bechtel.

The

PERSONAL TRAVEL SAFETY MANUAL

Security for
Business People
Traveling Overseas

CHRISTOPHER P. P. BARNES

TALLY HO
CONSULTING

THE PERSONAL TRAVEL SAFETY MANUAL
Security for Business People Traveling Overseas
Copyright © 2003 by Christopher P. P. Barnes

Published by
TALLY HO CONSULTING
PO Box 127, Nicasio, CA 94946, USA

Illustrations by Tom Wallerich, Mill Valley, California

ISBN 0-9740840-2-6
LCCN 2003093712

PRINTED IN THE USA
2 4 6 8 9 7 5 3 1

To
CATHERINE

Acknowledgements

*With thanks to Bryan Ray, Phil Gioia, Mort Grosser,
and others who provided inspiration for this book.*

Contents

Disclaimer

This manual is intended to provide information on travel safety. It offers tips and resources to prepare you for travel and to minimize the risks from crime. The author and publisher are not engaged in the provision of legal, medical, or self-defense services, and any advice given in these and other areas is merely offered for consideration by the reader. If legal, medical, or other expert opinion is required, the reader should refer to a competent professional in that field. Travel safety depends largely on common sense and on decisions made on the spot by the traveler.

CANTABIT VACUUS CORAM LATRONE VIATOR.

Travel light and you can sing in the robber's face.

— Juvenal, A.D. 60–130

Introduction

ACCORDING TO THE TRAVEL BROCHURES, overseas travel should be exciting, adventurous, and glamorous. The pessimist will say that it is exhausting and stressful, with the general issues of flying and the attendant hassles and delays. He will warn of crowded airports, security concerns, lost baggage, indifferent food, irritating fellow passengers, the possibility of catching an illness from one of them, jet lag, and possibly, at the far end, self-important foreign customs inspectors and surly immigration officials.

In addition to the travel itself, the getting there, there could be many stressful aspects of being there. To the same pessimist, these may include apparently incomprehensible foreign languages, different cultures, and the curious and possibly repugnant habits of the locals, as well as crime, corruption, and inadequate policing. Listen to these warnings and you might wonder why people go abroad at all!

In fact, the opportunity to travel quickly and easily from place to place around the world, to meet other peoples, explore different lands, and discover new cultures, is one of the greatest gifts of our age. International commerce thrives on the basis of face-to-face contacts and the consequent establishment of personal relationships between business people in different countries. No one should miss this opportunity through real or imagined concerns of inconvenience or of personal safety.

The secret to enjoying your travel and being safe is largely in the preparation and homework you do beforehand. All too often, the frantic businessman jets off to a conference in an exotic location, having no real idea about the country he is visiting, and the vacationer flies to an alluring tropical beach with no thought for the culture and lifestyle of the local inhabitants. Many travelers take too much luggage, yet forget something vital. Without doubt, whether you are a businessperson or a vacation traveler, you will have a far more rewarding experience if you are well prepared. Preparation will also reduce the stress of travel and, most importantly, make your journey considerably safer.

Since the attacks in New York and Washington of September 11, 2001, and subsequent terrorist events in Bali and elsewhere, the foremost concern of the contemporary traveler is personal security. In the past, many travelers have been blissfully unaware of security risks and personal safety precautions, and failed to take even the most elementary safeguards. People have traveled freely within the USA and to relatively safe "First World" countries for so long that they have become unconscious of the inherent risks abroad. The facts are that street crime and criminal assault are now common occurrences even in "civilized" countries, hate crime is on the rise, terrorism is now a global problem, and kidnapping for ransom is endemic in many Third World countries. American travelers are particularly at risk; they are seen as soft targets, are frequently easy to identify, are assumed to be relatively rich, and may be political targets because of their government's activities.

The chances of being directly affected by a random terrorist incident — though they are by their indiscriminate nature hard to guard against — are statistically low. On the other hand, crime, including violent crime, against business travelers and tourists has risen markedly in the past few years. Many of these crimes go unreported just because they happen abroad. Often the victim of an assault or robbery does not report the crime or wish to cooperate in a time-consuming criminal investigation overseas. More serious crimes go unreported for different reasons. Corporations that have had to pay ransoms, for instance, do not wish to advertise the fact, for fear of encouraging copycat crime. Corporate insurance premiums for hijack, kidnap, and ransom have risen astronomically, yet little effort is spent on awareness training and individual protection.

This Manual aims to teach the individual traveler how to prepare for an overseas journey, how to avoid problems, and how to behave if a problem does arise. Though the Manual is aimed primarily at the American overseas traveler, many of the lessons to be learned will be equally applicable to travel within the USA.

Each country is different in terms of threat and personal safety issues. Regarding street crime, as in the USA, most foreign cities have at least some areas that are considered unsafe and best avoided. In certain countries, where law and order is less than effective, kidnap is a known risk. Political strife in some countries manifests itself in terrorism or guerrilla warfare. Finally, though acts of terrorism can happen anywhere, they are more likely to occur in countries with ongoing internal conflicts, or countries where police control is limited. It is therefore imperative that you, the traveler, conduct a preliminary security assessment before departure to another country, and then make your own decision whether to travel and to what extent to adopt the relevant precautions discussed here.

The preventive measures you need to take will vary depending on your assessment of the threat; a visit to London will not merit the same concerns as a visit to Bogotá. Nonetheless, many of the low-level risks and basic safeguards discussed here will pertain everywhere, not only in Third World countries but also in developed countries, and even at home. This Manual aims to provide a good understanding of all levels of risk and related safety precautions.

In addition to the safeguards you take for an overseas or even domestic trip, it is important to first take care of the home front. One does not want to spend one's valuable time away worrying about the ranch, and it would be annoying to come home to a burgled house. Home security is therefore addressed here as part of the preparations for travel.

This is not a course in unarmed combat. There may or may not be the opportunity for self-defense in a robbery or kidnap situation. Nor is the purpose of this Manual to provide a country-by-country risk assessment. The aim is to show you how to best avoid the threat, or at least minimize the risk, in the first place.

Though this Manual is aimed at the individual, there is of course a corporate responsibility in respect of the management and care of the business traveler. Corporations ignore this responsibility at their peril, for the impact of failure to protect employees comes in legal liability, work outage, loss of reputation, medical costs, and effect on employee morale.

Throughout this Manual, travelers and criminals are referred to in the male gender, for ease of writing. Clearly, the hazards and precautions discussed apply equally, if not more so, to female travelers. Certain specifically female travel safety measures are addressed in a separate section for additional emphasis. Female criminals should not feel left out, either. The global rise in criminal and terrorist activity has been accompanied by a matching rise in female participation in crime; travelers should not over-look the threat of pick-pocketing, serious assault, terrorism, or other criminal activities from even the most innocent-looking females.

Whether you are a frequent business traveler who may have been lulled into a false sense of security, or a first-time vacation traveler, The Personal Travel Safety Manual will help you understand the threat and enable you to take precautions to reduce the risk.

THE THREAT

POVERTY, POLITICS, DRUGS, AND RELIGION all play a part in the root causes of crime and terrorism. The security threat varies from country to country and may vary within the country itself according to location, time of day, and other factors. It is important for every traveler to do some research and a risk assessment before setting out. Possible criminal threats can be categorized in four levels, as follows, with medical problems shown as a separate, fifth, category of risk to be considered.

COMMON CRIME

Common crime includes pickpocket attacks, bag snatching, theft, mugging, rape, car jacking, and armed robbery. Such incidents, though classified "common," are of course dangerous and can even prove fatal, usually where the victim offers resistance. Such crimes are especially typical of urban areas, from Lagos to London, and from New York to Sydney, and are the ones the business or vacation traveler is most likely to face.

High-level Crime

High-level crime includes kidnap, extortion, and murder. Kidnap for ransom has now become commonplace in several parts of Latin America and is an increasing problem in Eastern Europe, Russia, and elsewhere. At the low end of the scale, there have been many incidents of express kidnap whereby victims are abducted, robbed, taken to an ATM, and forced to withdraw and hand over their money, sometimes over several days. In other cases, victims have been held for months during protracted ransom negotiations.

Gangland shootings and murder are common in parts of many cities, including some in the USA.

Tribal allegiances and the power of local warlords in some countries such as Afghanistan and Yemen, undermine the power of central government and the rule of law outside the main cities. Kidnap and extortion are rife in the countryside.

Travelers must familiarize themselves with the sociopolitical situation of the country they are visiting, be aware of the incidence and type of criminal activity, understand the limits of police protection, and identify any "no-go" areas.

Terrorism

Assassination, kidnap, airplane hijacking, and bombings are some of the tools of the contemporary terrorist, whether religious fanatic or political extremist. Although it may not always be possible to avoid being in the wrong place at the wrong time, since the semi-random nature of terrorist attacks means that luck will play a part, you can certainly improve the odds for yourself. The first measure you can take is to avoid being singled out as someone worth kidnapping, whether express kidnapping as described above, or as part of a terrorist plot to raise ransom, or for some political aim. Maintaining a low profile to avoid becoming a target is discussed in the section below on Street Smarts.

Terrorist acts can happen in any country, but there are undoubtedly certain parts of the world where they can be considered a way of life. These countries are best avoided, or if you must visit them, the strictest precautions taken, particularly by steering clear of government buildings and public places frequented by foreigners, such as tourist restaurants, shopping malls, and nightclubs. Where kidnap is a known risk, consider using a professional protection service.

Terrorist acts are often conducted against groups or crowds for maximum impact. A terrorist bomb might be aimed at a particular grouping of people, such as American servicemen (the USS Cole in Yemen in 2000), or at buildings of note, such as the U.S. embassies in Kenya and Tanzania in 1998 and the World Trade Center in 2001.

Group kidnap for political ends, whether it is for a large ransom, a prisoner exchange bargaining chip, or other political ends, is another danger in some Third World countries. Group kidnapping may be attempted through the hijacking of a bus, plane, embassy, or even an entire public building.

A good understanding of the local political and military situations, together with personal vigilance and other precautions discussed below, may help you avoid being in that wrong place.

Insurgency

If you have to visit a country involved in an internal armed struggle or combating an insurrection, you will find that certain areas not controlled by the armed forces of the government are considered no-go areas, or at least dangerous to travel in. It is unlikely that these areas will be marked with hazard warnings. Be sure to establish in advance what the internal security situation is, and where the problem areas are so that, unless you are an accredited war correspondent, you can keep well clear of any conflict. The risks of getting too close are evident: you could get shot, you could get blown up on a mine, you might get kidnapped or arrested, and you could be suspected and accused of spying or aiding one side or the other. If you do have a reason to be in or near a war zone, even if it is not officially designated as such, get an official pass and, if appropriate, suitable military transport and armed escort.

Risks to travelers from insurgency situations are limited to specific known countries, and appropriate precautions can be taken. The threat to the public from acts of terrorism is real and present, but statistically the chance of being involved in a terrorist incident while traveling is still remote. The greatest risk to travelers, and a rising problem, is the danger of getting involved in common but possibly violent crime. This Manual focuses on threat assessment, preparations, precautions, and actions to limit and avoid these risks.

Medical Problems

Sickness is a high-priority security concern since a sick traveler is not alert, is likely to appear defenseless, and is therefore more prone to attack than a clearly healthy person. Consideration of health risks, avoidance of disease, prevention of accidents, and the appropriate precautions, are therefore important aspects of the risk analysis and travel preparation covered in this Manual.

Corporate Responsibility and Management

Responsibility and Liability

Corporate responsibility for employee safety while traveling is an area that many American companies have, until recently, largely ignored. Yet failure to protect employees exposes the corporation to considerable liability when things go wrong, including loss of earnings, lawsuits, loss of reputation, and long-term personnel problems. These can have an immediate impact on shareholder value, and possibly put a company out of business. Thus management responsibility includes travel safety training, continuous risk evaluation and monitoring, control of employee travel, and crisis management.

A corporation must, therefore, conduct its own international threat assessments for all countries in which its employees are working or traveling, and continuously monitor each local situation to update those assessments. Based on these, management must issue and maintain regular travel guidelines. In areas of high risk, managers must decide whether business travel is essential and advisable, or whether the business aim can be achieved by other means such as computer conferencing, teleconferencing, or video-conferencing.

High-risk Areas

If employees are being sent to a very high-risk area, where insurgency or kidnap are prevalent, State Department and other warnings must be carefully considered, professional security advice must be sought, and tight controls imposed on employees' movement and activity within the country concerned.

In this case, employees should be trained in defensive driving, anti-hijack, and anti-kidnap precautions. Business operations in high-risk areas may require covert or overt protection, ranging from the use of armed bodyguards and "discrete" armor-protected limousines, to escorted armed convoys and movement by helicopter. In such a high-risk environment, a secure base or compound will most likely be required, rather than a public hotel.

Risk Monitoring

The corporation must monitor and keep itself informed on security risks in all countries to which it sends employees. Management must ensure that employees are kept fully informed of the threat, that they are trained in travel safety, and that, ultimately, the individual has the option not to travel. This Manual should form part of such an employees' training package.

MANAGEMENT OF TRAVELING EMPLOYEES

The corporation must track all traveling employees, know where each one is at all times, and be able to contact them instantly in an emergency. This requirement implies keeping detailed travel plans for all employees, including air travel, in-country transportation, hotel details (phone and fax), local contact details, and employee contact details, including cell-phone numbers, e-mail addresses, voice mailbox, and in-country business-contact data.

INSURANCE

Employers must provide travel healthcare coverage, including emergency medical evacuation provisions, for employees who travel abroad, and must ensure that they receive appropriate vaccinations and medical advice well in advance of their travels. In addition, there must be clear guidelines for the procedure to be followed in case of employee medical emergency overseas.

Where employees are to be sent on a business trip or expatriate assignment to a country with a high incidence of kidnap*, then K & R (Kidnap and Ransom) insurance should be arranged. Most major insurers offer K & R insurance. A policy typically covers the cost of negotiation as well as payment of the ransom. It should be noted, however, that management should keep K & R insurance details confidential, lest the notion of almost limitless funds actually attract kidnappers.

---

* Colombia, Mexico, Brazil, and Chechnya have the highest incidence of kidnap, accounting for 90 percent of kidnaps for ransom.

CRISIS MANAGEMENT

Detailed crisis management is a topic beyond the scope of this Manual, but in brief, the corporation must be prepared to handle any crisis incident, including problems affecting employees overseas. A crisis could be any major event, such as an earthquake, a hostage situation, outbreak of war, facilities fire, or a terrorist attack on company personnel or facilities.

A Crisis Management Team (CMT) should be a designated unit in every company, with tried and tested operating procedures in place. Emergency communications, together with recall and evacuation plans for overseas personnel, form an important part of these operating procedures. A CMT would normally include a senior manager at board level, and a representative from each of Human Resources, Security, Travel Management, Legal, and Marketing Communications departments, the last for management of news releases and press interfaces.

All of this implies careful planning, frequently updated written procedures, continuous management oversight, and regular training of management and employees.

Research and Preparations

Risk Analysis

A TOP-LEVEL ASSESSMENT OF THE RISKS in travel to any country includes careful consideration of political stability, international relations (particularly with the USA), review of recent and present border disputes, insurgency or civil unrest, religious strife, recent history of terrorist activity, and the level of organized crime, including kidnap.

Additionally, any specific geographical trouble zones or no-go areas must be identified, and the viability of the security forces and police to provide protection assessed. The security and safety of roads and airports is of course a primary concern in this risk analysis.

Background, Geography, Politics, and People

Make sure you are fully briefed before you travel. Even if you are traveling as part of a group, remember that you might get separated at some stage, so you cannot rely on your partner or business colleague to lead you around. Besides, they may not have done their own research thoroughly. Do your homework before traveling and you will have a much more rewarding experience and avoid a lot of stress. The first step is to get a map and study the geography and topography of the country. Even if you are only visiting the capital city, it pays to put your intended destination in perspective. If you're traveling more widely, it is vital to know where you are going and how you are going to get there.

Read a history of the country to understand its development, as well as external influences such as a colonial past or wars with neighbors.

You can get information from the Internet or your local library, particularly data on population, ethnic and religious groupings, system of government, languages spoken, economic situation, and climatic conditions.

If there is a known internal security problem, such as an insurgency, going on in the country you plan to visit, it is wise to get an understanding of the political background and underlying causes, as well as the geographic extent and scope of any fighting. Clearly, you do not want to drive blithely into the middle of a firefight or a guerrilla-held area.

A travel guidebook can provide additional country background as well as suggestions on hotels, but should not be relied on for a threat assessment. For one thing, travel guidebooks are only as up to date as their latest revision; for another, they are in the business of encouraging travel and selling books.

Find out what the options are for travel within your destination country, whether public transport is safe there, whether driving yourself is an option, and whether any areas are unsafe or off limits.

Buying a phrase book will allow you to learn at least a few key phrases.

Reading the international sections of the U.S. newspapers and international periodicals such as the Economist and Financial Times Foreign Affairs will offer a feel for the current local political and economic situation. Your research should help you to understand the local issues and to be aware of local sensitivities.

Also, you need to visit the Web site of the U.S. consulate or embassy, note the local address and phone numbers, and check there for any relevant travel advice.

Intelligence Gathering before Travel

Do your homework before you travel, in order to understand the local situation. Analyze the situation, assess the risk and be prepared. The more thorough your preparation, the better prepared and safer you will be.

Check on current information and travel advisories with the State Department by visiting their excellent Web site, http://travel.state.gov/ or by calling 202 647-5225. Look up the Consular Information Sheet for the country or countries on your itinerary. Consular Information Sheets for each country do not provide advice, but they describe entry and visa requirements and currency, and provide information about crime and security, political disturbances, and driving. This is also the place to find the contact details for the embassy and consulates.

Check for any relevant Travel Advisories or Public Announcements at the same State Department Web site. These provide specific country alert information or travel warnings in case of any particular threat.

Check the Overseas Security Advisory Council Web site also, http://www.ds-osac.org/.

You can cross-calibrate the information provided, by checking similar travel advisory services from other nations, such as Britain's Foreign Office site, http://www.fco.gov.uk/ or Australia's, http://www.dfat.gov.au/consular/advice/.

For background information on any country, visit the CIA Fact Book: http://www.cia.gov/cia/publications/factbook/.

Check the travel books and sources at your local library, as well as newspapers and periodicals, for relevant current events and political angles. Most libraries also offer travel videos, which will give you ideas on dress and customs.

Check in advance with the U.S. embassy or consulate in the country you plan to visit, for any specific local problems, security threats, and recommended precautions. Such information is often available at the appropriate embassy Web site, or you can write to them or call in advance. U.S. Consular Affairs officers (Foreign Service Professionals) are charged with protecting the interests, health and safety of American nationals abroad.

At the same time, check with the embassy for any specific laws that might affect you, such as import restrictions and driving regulations.

If you are visiting business acquaintances or friends overseas, do not fail to ask for their perspective on safety, as well as recommendations on places to stay and places to avoid.

LANGUAGE, CUSTOMS AND CULTURE

If you plan to visit a country where a foreign language is spoken, get a phrase book and learn a few key phrases. If time allows, take a language course. A single semester of a weekly evening language class at a local college will pay huge dividends. Most foreigners will appreciate any attempt you make to speak their language. In addition, if you can understand at least some of what is being spoken around you, and recognize a few of the more common written signs and phrases, you will be more productive, more in tune with your environment, and in the final analysis considerably safer.

You can unwittingly cause offense in many countries, and you will certainly display your ignorance, unless you make an effort to check the culture in advance. In some countries it is rude to touch a person's head; even patting a child on the head will give offense. In other countries it is rude to sit cross-legged or to show the soles of the shoes or feet. In many countries, men may not strike up a conversation with a woman they do not know.

The way you dress can also cause offense. Muslim countries, for instance, are particularly sensitive to ladies displaying too much flesh, and to do so can risk a street altercation, beating, or arrest. Refer to the section on Muslim Countries elsewhere in this Manual for more specific advice. Even Western European countries are typically more formal in their dress. Wearing jeans and sneakers to the theater or opera may be comfortable, but is likely to show you up as an "Ugly American" in many capital cities.

KNOW THE LAW

You will be subject to the legislation and legal system of the country you are visiting, and ignorance of the law is never an excuse, so check for any unusual laws. Alcohol, for instance, is banned in certain countries, while possession of firearms is against the law in many. Possession of illegal drugs can lead to imprisonment in most countries, and the death penalty in some.

Check opinions on whether the police can be relied on or are ineffective, and whether police corruption is rife, as this may affect your course of action if you run into problems.

The Local Map

Get a street map covering the city or cities you plan to visit. Study it in advance and familiarize yourself with your area of interest, particularly the streets around your hotel and around any places you plan to visit, as well as landmarks and other key points.

As an exercise, try reproducing the main streets and landmarks from memory. Check your drawing against the map and then try again until you have established a good mental picture. On foot, you will not want to be marked as a tourist by constantly checking your map in public. If you plan on being driven somewhere, you need to know that you are on course for your intended destination, not just being taken for a ride or hijacked! When driving yourself you need a good understanding of the geography, topography, and landmarks, if not the precise route, without constantly stopping to refer to a map.

If you intend to drive yourself, find out in advance about local road signs, symbols, and language: they might not be in English, and might not even be in a script you can decipher. Also, check on local traffic regulations, such as which side of the street to drive on, and any special right-of-way laws. It is surprising how many visitors to the United Kingdom, for example, are shocked to find the traffic driving on the left side of the road, the steering wheel on the right side of their rental car, and that coping with the left-handed gear stick requires some unaccustomed manual dexterity!

Incidentally, a frequent cause of accidents to pedestrian visitors in "left-side-of-the-road" countries is from stepping off the curb without looking right. This lamentable lack of awareness is occasionally fatal.

As a driver you will also want to know about any road and bridge tolls and how toll booths operate. You should plan to have suitable coins or change available in your car to drive through such toll stations without delay.

Remember, if you drive a car in a foreign country it is your responsibility to drive within the law—their law! You may be jet-lagged, confused, unused to the speed of traffic, unclear on the meaning of road signs, unsure of the right of way, in an unfamiliar car, and lost. It is often better to get to your hotel initially by limousine and avoid the hassles and danger of driving rental cars until you have settled in to the country, got over the jet lag, and become attuned to local driving conditions.

Check whether you can drive on an International Driving Permit (IDP) in the country you are visiting. Purchase one anyway for use as an identification document when you do not want to hand over a passport, as the IDP is written in several languages and is more easily replaced than a passport or state driver's license if lost or confiscated. The IDP is available through the American Automobile Association for a small fee.

DOUBLE PRECAUTIONS

It is recommended that you avoid traveling abroad alone if possible. Two pairs of eyes are better than one, and two people can look after each other much better and will present less of a target for random crime. For instance, one can guard baggage while the other is arranging a car at the airport. One can navigate while the other drives. If one gets sick, the other can provide care and obtain appropriate assistance. Two people together are much less likely to be attacked or pick-pocketed than one, especially if they look aware and assertive. Plan to travel with a partner if possible.

MEDICAL PREPARATIONS

Medical emergencies can ruin a vacation or a business trip. Travelers are particularly prone to accidents and diseases during and immediately following a trip abroad. There are several reasons for this. One is the prevalence of airborne germs and poor air quality in airplanes, together with the chance of one or more passengers passing on an infection. A second reason is jet lag, which induces fatigue and reduces immunity to disease. Accidents, particularly driving accidents, are often attributed to jet lag. A third reason is the prevalence of different microorganisms and diseases in foreign countries, which our bodies are unused to fending off.

As mentioned above, sickness is a major security concern because a sick traveler is not alert and may appear defenseless, and is thus more at risk of assault than an evidently healthy person. Get regular checkups if you are a frequent traveler; if you go abroad only occasionally, get a checkup before you go.

As part of your preparations you should check with the Center for Disease Control to see what particular health risks prevail in the country you plan to visit, http://www.cdc.gov/.

Check well in advance for any required or recommended vaccinations, and get them in time to be effective; this may mean several weeks before departure. Vaccinations for underdeveloped countries may include Hepatitis A and B, Cholera, Yellow Fever, and others. Do not be tempted to ignore the recommendations; some of these diseases can have long-lasting effects on your health—if they do not kill you immediately. Keep the certificates with your passport or you may be obliged to get another vaccination, either upon arrival or when you return to the USA from an infected region.

Make sure you have an up-to-date tetanus shot; tetanus can be contracted from small wounds and is frequently fatal. Medical facilities overseas might not meet your expectations in terms of skill or hygiene; it is therefore best to avoid the need to use them in the first place!

If visiting a malarial area, get advice from a qualified doctor* on appropriate anti-malarial drugs. Typically, a course of anti-malarial drugs starts a couple of weeks prior to departure and continues for several weeks after your exit from a malarial area. If you do not take the full course you can still contract malaria, and without diagnosis and treatment it can kill you. Malaria is spread by mosquitoes, so plan on taking some repellent and even a mosquito net with you.

Take reading glasses if you use them, as well as a spare pair. Sunglasses and sun hats are also important in some climates. Sun burn and heat exhaustion can be debilitating, making you more vulnerable to criminal assault, while of course heat stroke can be fatal.

Drinking contaminated water can result in serious illnesses such as typhoid or Hepatitis A, a viral infection of the liver. If

---

* Your family doctor may not be an expert in tropical diseases and precautions, but should be able to refer you to someone who is.

you expect to spend any time in a remote area where safe water or bottled drinks may not be available, take a water purification system with you, both a filtration unit and tablets. You can buy these in the USA at any outdoor sporting goods store.

Check that your medical insurance is up to date and covers you for the countries you are visiting. Find out what the emergency medical procedure is while traveling. Do you have to get pre-approval for a hospital visit? Is there a recommended list of hospitals and English-speaking doctors? Make sure your medical insurance includes Emergency Medical Evacuation, and that you know how to activate it in case of a dire medical emergency. You might not be satisfied with the level of emergency medical skill in Timbuktu!

Pack a basic first aid and medication kit. A recommended list is attached in Appendix D. Your kit should include any special medications you are currently taking, and enough to cover an extended stay (but not so much that you could be accused of trafficking!). If you take along prescription medications, make sure they are in their original, clearly labeled dispensers. If they are unusual or contain narcotics, obtain a certificate or letter of explanation from your doctor. For such exotic medications check with the consulate of the country you intend to visit before arrival to make sure there is no ban on importing your prescription drug.

Air quality is extremely poor in certain cities around the world, due to vehicle exhaust fumes, smoke from forest fires, coal fires, and other hazards, depending on the season. Visitors and residents are prone to bronchial and respiratory problems. Although you may be conducting your business in an air-conditioned and filtered environment, you may want to take along a few disposable hygiene facemasks for protection outdoors. You can also use these masks in the plane or crowded areas to protect yourself from viral infections; it may look silly, but at least you will stay healthy.

Never take illegal drugs to a foreign country. Customs officials are always on the lookout for people carrying illegal drugs, and the penalties can be severe. Even small amounts of drugs can result in imprisonment. In some countries mere possession carries a death penalty.

Finally, do not set off on a journey overseas if you are already sick. Flying is likely to worsen your condition, and you will be more of a target for criminals if you appear weak and defenseless.

Flight Plans

Select nonstop flights where possible, for safety reasons. If you have to stage, try to use the same airline, as there is less chance of losing your checked-in baggage.

If you are staging through another country, make sure it is not a hostile one or in the throes of a revolution or insurgency. It is not unknown for individual passengers to be abducted from a plane during a stopover.

Choose your flights to arrive at your destination in the daytime and with sufficient time to get to your hotel in daylight, even if this means an additional stopover on the way. Night arrivals and movement can be confusing in a foreign country, and there is an increased risk of crime if you arrive after dark.

If your itinerary does not allow for a daytime arrival, consider using a good airport hotel, if there is one close to your destination. Then you can complete your journey in safety the following day.

Visas

Some countries require a visa to be stamped in your passport prior to arrival. Check with your airline or travel agent to establish whether you need an advance visa for the country you are visiting. At the same time, make sure your passport is valid for at least six months. Some countries will refuse you entry if your passport is close to expiration.

If a visa is required, obtain it — usually by submitting your passport, additional passport photos, a visa fee, and an application form directly to that country's consulate in the USA — well before your intended travel date. There are companies that specialize in procuring visas. They handle your passport, get the forms and fees to the relevant consulate, and expedite the process through to getting your passport and visa back into your hands. They charge a modest fee, which is generally well worth the money.

Travel Plan in Country

Before you leave home, work out in detail where you are going after you have landed at your destination airport, and exactly how you are going to get there. In the first instance, you need to plan how to get safely to your hotel or other accommodation, and then decide how you are going to travel around, whether by public transport or rental car, for instance. This is largely a function of the security situation. Buses are dangerous in some countries, and driving oneself is a risky venture in others. Official taxis may be fine; if not, the hotel limousine service may serve. In a high-risk country or situation, an armor-protected vehicle should be used, with a trusted driver who has been properly trained in defensive driving techniques.

If you decide it is safe to drive yourself and you plan to rent a car, ask when you make your reservation exactly where the car-rental desk and pickup locations are at the arrival airport. Have the rental company send you a map of the airport facilities in advance. Ask whether there is a shuttle bus to the rental parking area, and if so, how the bus is marked and where it stops relative to your arrival terminal.

Ask whether the rental company will deliver the car to your hotel a day or two after your arrival. If so, that is usually the most sensible way to proceed, as it spares you the dangers of driving a strange car in a foreign country on your first day there.

Some countries require you to hold an International Driving Permit (IDP) with your regular license. Check with the rental company. As noted elsewhere, it is not a bad idea to have one in any case.

If you intend to drive yourself in a foreign country, study their Highway Code and road signs in advance. Study the map of your routes carefully, especially if you intend to drive from the airport to your first night's accommodation. Don't wait until you're driving to have to stop and read the map or to check the meaning of a road sign.

If you intend to drive from one part of the country to another, plan your routes and alternatives, identify the best stops, and book suitable hotels before leaving home. You can always update your ideas and change the plan in country from the safety of your first hotel — remembering, of course, to let your home contacts know of any changes.

If you will be traveling by car, make your car-emergency plan in advance. What will you do if the car breaks down in the countryside? In town? What formal roadside assistance is available, if any? What safe alternative transport will be available? Check the recommended breakdown procedures with the rental company.

SELECTION OF A SECURE HOTEL

Security is the most important factor in selecting a hotel. You need to be able to relax in a secure base, or you'll be at risk and under stress the whole trip. All these factors play a part:

Quality

Do not be tempted to stay in a budget hotel overseas. Use quality hotels where available, particularly in cities where security is known to be poor.

Location

Make sure the hotel is in a good location, in a business area or smart neighborhood, which is likely to be better policed. If in doubt, ask the airline which hotel they use. Flight crews usually stay in a major hotel with good security.

Convenience

Keep your local travel to a minimum by choosing a hotel close to the businesses you are visiting, or, if you are a tourist, close to the main sights you plan to see.

Hotel Security

Security is usually best at major hotels, as they can afford appropriate physical security measures and security staff. Even if you are traveling on a tight budget, you still need to get the most secure hotel you can afford; consider the alternative! Review the hotels accredited by your airline. Ask your local contact, if you have one, about recommended hotels and their security record. You can ask the U.S. embassy or consulate security staff for their recommendations. You can also ask them whether any hotel you are considering has been the subject of any recent security incidents or complaints by American tourists or business travelers.

Before you make a hotel reservation, call and check the security features listed below. You should ask to speak to the security manager—that way, you know they have one. (If you feel uncomfortable about asking these questions, imagine that you're reviewing security for a presidential visit. Then ask yourself whether your own safety is any less important.)

- Is the lobby always manned?

- Is the front door guarded?

- Are other hotel entrances secure, and locked at night?

- Are security staff on duty 24/7?

- Are the room keys electronic?

- Do the room doors have dead bolts and peepholes?

- Are room safes provided? If not, is a hotel safe available?

- Are smoke detectors and sprinklers installed on every floor and in every room?*

- Is there hotel limousine service, with English-speaking drivers and airport collection service?

---

* Some fire experts, at the risk of appearing paranoid, recommend packing your own portable smoke detector, and even a smoke hood.

If you have a car, make sure that secure, well-lit parking is located within the hotel and that valet parking service is available.

Make sure your needed facilities are available inside the hotel (including restaurants, fitness center, business center) to minimize your need to go outside the security of the hotel.

Finally, having researched and found yourself the right hotel, make a reservation, and keep a note of the reservation number.

Packing for Safety

Pack a small carry-on bag or briefcase with the bare essentials for your visit. This would include passport, tickets, essential medication, glasses, itinerary and contact list, laptop or PDA, business cards, and business documents, etc. A suggested list is at Appendix A.

Pack a separate suitcase to check in, containing all nonessentials (which you can afford to lose and can easily be replaced), clothes, shoes, toiletries, books, and so on (see Appendix B). Remember that scissors, pocketknives, and any sharp objects must be in your check-in suitcase, not in a carry-on bag, from which they are likely to be confiscated. Do not take more luggage than you need; not only are you more likely to get robbed with a lot of luggage, but it can be an impediment in an emergency.

Do not pack any sensitive company information in your check-in baggage, whether in document or data form. In fact, you should make sure you are not taking abroad any information that is not directly needed for your trip. Many companies have lost control of their intellectual property through negligence. If you lose a laptop containing the source code for your next-generation software product, or the designs for the next Stealth fighter, your own future at your company, and indeed the company's own survival, may be in doubt.

Ostentatious, expensive looking suitcases or briefcases mark you as a target. Use sturdy, low-key luggage. An obvious laptop bag or camera case is also an inviting target for a thief. Mark both your suitcase and your carry-on bag with colored bands, decals, or other clear marks, both for easy identification and so that you can see if someone else grabs them from the airport carousel or X-ray machine.

Label your bags with the minimum information required: your name and initials and an office or PO Box address, but not the street address of your unoccupied house! Neither your company name, nor your exalted title need appear, nor indeed your first name . Make sure the label is covered to conceal the information from unauthorized eyes. Put a duplicate contact label on the inside of the case.

Pack only what you need. Do not take unneeded credit cards or documents with you. Pack your own bags and, especially while abroad, make sure no one has an opportunity to insert anything into them. You do not want a drug dealer using one of your bags and you as an unwitting courier, or a terrorist slipping a bomb on board courtesy of your luggage.

Do not pack a firearm unless you have first obtained a permit from the country you are visiting. Unregistered firearms are illegal in most countries (including Mexico and Canada) and the penalties for carrying them can be severe. The same applies to large knives, such as hunting knives, which may be illegal.

If you are taking newspapers or periodicals from home that you might leave on the plane or at your destination, remove your name and address from them before you set out.

Lock your baggage with a sturdy lock. This will not stop a determined thief, but will deter the casual thief and the opportunistic robber.

Before leaving Home

Home Security

THE BEST SECURITY MEASURE IN LEAVING YOUR HOME is to have it occupied by a house sitter or relative, but if your home will be unoccupied you must take all possible measures to make sure it is secure. All windows and doors must be locked, the alarm system, if you have one, activated, all ladders and tools locked inside the garage or shed. If you have outdoor lights operated by motion sensors, make sure they are in good working order.

Cancel the newspaper, mail and other deliveries so that they do not pile up outside your home making your absence very obvious. Leave a car outside to make your home appear occupied. It may be cheaper to lose a car than to have your home burgled. Put a couple of internal lights and a radio on timers to make the home appear occupied. Close the drapes so people cannot see in.

Tell a trusted neighbor that you will be away. Ask him or her to report to the police any suspicious activity, such as the arrival of a large van at your house. Leave your contact details with the neighbor so they can tell you, too. If your house has a burglar alarm, and you have no house sitter, make sure the neighbor knows what to do if it alarms, such as contacting the police, and how to switch off the alarm once the premises have been checked.

Tell the local police that the house will be unoccupied, and leave them an emergency contact number for a friend or relative as well as the contact details of your trusted neighbor. Do not expect the police to try to call you overseas.

Guard your itinerary even before you leave home. There is no need to broadcast your intended absence. Tell only the people who need to know; everyone else can hear about it when you return.

If you live in an urban area, plan to have a friend drive you to your departure airport, rather than advertising your imminent departure by having a taxi come to your house.

Personal Administration

Make sure you have an up-to-date will, and give a close relative or friend a power of attorney to deal with your affairs. If you get detained in a crisis overseas, you do not want to be worrying about routine home administration.

Make photocopies of your passport, airline ticket, credit cards, traveler's check serial numbers, driver's license, and other documents. These copies can be left at your office or with a friend in case the originals are lost or stolen during your trip. If any of these documents do get lost, a copy can then quickly be faxed to you if required, which will make it a lot easier to get a replacement. Write down the direct phone numbers—not toll-free numbers, which do not work from abroad—of the issuing airlines, banks, and credit-card companies, so you know whom to call if they are lost or stolen. Refer to the checklist in Appendix E.

Remove unnecessary items from your wallet, such as extra credit cards. Remove old labels from your suitcases.

Leave your expensive watch and jewelry at home, secured in a wall safe or a bank vault. Do not even wear an expensive-looking watch—it might look expensive and attractive to a thief; even worse, a criminal who finds he has just stolen a fake watch may be more inclined to violence.

Make sure there is sufficient credit on the credit cards you are taking to cover your trip abroad, including an extended stay or emergency travel. Running out of cash and credit abroad can be embarrassing at the least.

Write out a detailed travel plan and leave copies with your office and a close friend or relative. This should include your flight itineraries; your hotels (with addresses, phone numbers, fax numbers, and reservation numbers); your cell-phone number and e-mail address, your car-rental agency (location, phone number, and reservation numbers); and your local itinerary, including detailed internal travel plan and route, with contact names and numbers. Tell your office staff and relatives to keep your travel information confidential and not to divulge it to anyone who does not have a real need to know. You don't want unauthorized people knowing that your home is unoccupied, nor do you want unexpected visitors in your hotel room overseas.

Arrange for your destination hotel's transport service or your local business contact to meet you at the airport upon arrival.

Make sure you discuss how and where to find and identify your contact at the airport and what to do if the plane is delayed. Do not allow someone at the destination airport to plan to hold up a board with your name or company name on it; use the driver's name or a predetermined local alias on a signboard, and have a password or phrase agreed upon in advance. Ingenious robbers have been known to copy a name sign at an airport arrival hall and pose as the official driver, intending to relieve the unwary traveler of his suitcase.

If you plan to drive yourself, reserve a car, note the confirmation number, and find out precisely how to get to the rental office desk at your destination. Refer to the section below on rental cars, especially the cautions contained therein.

Get an International Driving Permit. If you are asked to show identification or a driver's license, use your IDP, as it is written in several languages, and being more easily replaced than a passport, should not impact your journey if lost or confiscated.

If you are taking your laptop or personal digital assistant (PDA), back it up before leaving home. Remove any sensitive or personal data from it, especially personal, financial, and password information. Get an encryption program and activate it, so that if you close down or leave your laptop or PDA unused for more than a couple of minutes, the data is encrypted. This is considerably more secure than mere password protection.

Contact List

Make two lists, the first a short list of home contacts to take with you, including names, phone numbers, and e-mail addresses of both business and personal contacts. Make a second list of contacts in your destination country, including your hotels, your primary business contacts, the embassy or consulate, the local airline office, the local phone number for the car-rental office (together with a note of your reservation number), and the local access number for U.S. phone service (such as AT&T Direct). Get a couple of home numbers for local contacts in the country you are visiting, such as a trusted business contact, so that if you get in trouble over an evening or weekend you have someone nearby to call for assistance. This list can be on your laptop or PDA if you carry one, but keep a printout back at your home or office in case you lose the laptop.

Emergency Card

Use the contact list to make a short emergency contact list on a small card. On this card, include your name, blood type, and details of your designated emergency contact person. Add your key local contacts (business and personal), as well as local phone numbers for police, the U.S. embassy, your hotel, car-rental company local office, and so on (see Appendix C). Plan to carry this emergency card with you at all times.

Money

Get some cash in the local currency for the country or countries you plan to visit. You might be able to get this at your departure airport, but it is usually more reliable to get it earlier at a bank. Note that your local bank will require some advance notice if you plan on getting foreign currency. As a minimum, get enough cash to cover your first two days' cash expenses, including local transportation and tips. Avoid carrying too much cash or large denominations.

Get familiar with the local currency and its value. You do not want to be obviously figuring out the exchange rate every time you make a purchase, or displaying all your bank notes in order to select the correct denomination. Giving someone a fistful of money and saying, "Help yourself" is, of course, the ultimate recipe for disaster.

Automatic Teller Machines (ATMs), compatible with major banking chains, are now available in most countries around the world and are a convenient way of drawing additional cash in country. They might, of course, not be available in more remote locations, in which case a stock of traveler's checks should be taken.

Traveler's checks are in any case a good standby for foreign travel. Sign them as soon as you get them, and keep duplicate records of the serial numbers, one with you and the other at home. Unlike cash, they are insured if you lose them. You can cash them with your counter-signature and supporting identity document at a bank, or commonly at your hotel.

Take a spare identity document, such as an old driver's license or other official-looking card with a photo on it, if you have one. Some overseas businesses and government agencies require you to lodge an identity card at the gate while visiting, and you can usually lodge an old or dispensable card rather than risk losing your passport.

Support Services

Make a note of the location and telephone number of the U.S. embassy or consulate, as well as similar facilities in the area belonging to other friendly nations. If you plan to spend some time in a country where a volatile political situation pertains, it is worth ensuring that the embassy can contact you in case of specific alerts; other friendly embassies can at least provide a safe haven if you have a safety problem in their vicinity. When visiting a high- or medium-risk country, call or visit the U.S. embassy or consulate upon arrival to get a security update and to register your contact details, including your hotel and local business and cell phone details, along with your intended departure date.

COMMUNICATIONS

CELL PHONES

ACQUIRE A CELL PHONE THAT WORKS in the country you are visiting. Many countries in Europe, Asia, and the Middle East use the digital Groupe Speciale Mobile or GSM standard for mobile telephony, which is not compatible with regular U.S. cell phones. However, a GSM phone from one country can typically be used in any other GSM country provided the international roaming feature is set.* GSM phones can also be rented for Europe and certain other areas before leaving the USA. You can find suppliers via the Internet. Make sure a spare battery and suitable AC charger are included, as well as a car cigarette-lighter charger.

---

* This roaming facility can get expensive: for instance, if you acquire your service in France and use your phone in South Africa. Frequent business travelers may find it worth purchasing a GSM phone without any associated service and then buying a "SIM" card (which provides the phone number) and prepaid phone minutes in each GSM country visited. Additional prepaid phone minutes can be bought later as necessary.

In many countries, you can rent a cell phone at the arrival airport. This should be a last resort; the fewer activities you need to conduct upon arrival, before getting yourself and your baggage to the safety of your hotel, the better. On the subject of cell phone usage, you should be aware that in many countries it is illegal to use a cell phone while driving a car.

Keep a record of your cell phone number, as well as the serial number, in case it gets stolen. Make a note of the phone number of the cell phone service provider in the country you are visiting, so you can cancel the service if the phone is stolen.

Program into your cell phone's memory the emergency numbers, including the local police and the U.S. embassy or consulate. (9-1-1 is not the emergency number in most countries.)

Your hotel may also be able to help in a travel emergency, at least by sending out a car and an interpreter, so program your hotel phone number into the speed-dial facility of your cell phone.

Pay Phones

Whether you have a cell phone or not, familiarize yourself with the local public telephone system. If your cell phone is lost or snatched you may need to use a call box, and the instructions might not be in English! Be sure at all times to carry a prepaid phone card, or enough coins to make emergency calls from a call box.

Communication Plan

Make a formal communications plan and discuss it before you depart. Arrange to call in to home or office, or to e-mail regularly on an agreed schedule (at least daily), making certain your business associates and relatives know and understand the plan.

Decide what should be done (and by whom) if you fail to call in on schedule. Agree upon a code word or phrase to use to indicate a dire emergency; if someone is forcing you to make a phone call, you need to be able to communicate that fact.

The communications plan must be two-way. It is important for your safety that people at home also know how to get hold of you; for instance, they might be able to alert you to a local crisis before you hear about it yourself.

COMMUNICATIONS SECURITY

This is a subject that is often overlooked, but international commercial and economic espionage is now a way of life. You should assume that the hotel operator monitors, at least casually, all telephone conversations from your hotel room. In addition, your work may be of interest to other parties, particularly if you are working on classified government contracts, high-dollar-value projects, or with unique technology. In addition to the commercial or economic threats, it is possible that something you say incautiously on the telephone may be relayed to a criminal and could set you up as a target.

Assume also that all documents you discard in your hotel waste bin will be reassembled and reviewed later by the local intelligence agency, and the details passed on to interested local government agencies or your competitors.

If your work is of interest to the government of the country you are visiting, to influential local firms, or to sophisticated foreign competitors, your hotel telephone conversations will very likely be comprehensively recorded and analyzed. In addition, your e-mail through a hotel data network may routinely be scrutinized by the host country's intelligence agency. Fax messages are, of course, totally insecure. Whether you are visiting a Third World country or an unscrupulous Western ally, you should always assume that someone is monitoring your hotel communications.

In addition to telephone tapping, a bug may be placed in your room itself if you or your business is of particular interest to the host country. Advances in technology and miniaturization make it impractical to sweep a hotel room for bugs without sophisticated equipment, and even then impossible to keep it clear because of the number of people that have access to a hotel room and could introduce another bug. Therefore, if your business is sensitive, do not discuss details on the phone or hold confidential discussions in your room with a business colleague. Your local office if you have one, or the embassy, might be better equipped to provide an electronically secure environment. You can also hold discussions while walking outside (assuming it is safe to do so) and in restaurants selected at random at the last minute. Although directional microphones could be used to pick up your conversation, the effort required for such surveillance probably exceeds the gains to be made, as far as a foreign intelligence agency is concerned.

Do not hold sensitive business discussions in the hotel limousine or taxi. Many business executives assume the driver speaks little English or is not interested in their conversation. In fact, he might speak English, but even if he doesn't, he could be employed by a competitor or the host government to tape-record your conversations.

A digital mobile phone is far more secure than the previous generation analog cell phones, but use it away from your hotel room or any conference room, as you are still susceptible there to the electronic room bug.

E-mail is the easiest communications channel to secure, through various commercially available, high-grade encryption programs. Just be careful not to compose your confidential messages anywhere that you can be observed by a long-range camera. The commercials showing the executive reclining with a laptop under a palm tree on the beach fail to show the spy in the background with the telephoto lens. Make sure you check the U.S. rules on exporting your chosen encryption program, and that you will not be infringing your host nation's laws by employing cryptography.

If you are concerned about privacy, then communications security precautions must be planned from the outset. Unnecessary discussions or reports should be avoided. For example, do not send a detailed written or verbal status report back to the home office if it can wait until you get out of the country.

DEFENSIVE TRAVEL

PERSONAL AWARENESS

THE MOST IMPORTANT TOOL IN PERSONAL SECURITY is vigilance. Be aware of your surroundings, the atmosphere, and the people around you at all times. Be alert for danger, and look sharp. Whether traveling or relaxing, do not become engrossed in your thoughts in public, or in a conversation with your partner, to the exclusion of your surroundings.

Pickpockets and muggers are always on the lookout for an easy target, someone who is clearly not looking out for himself. Do not stroll around in public with a Walkman over your ears, or loiter talking loudly on your cell phone. Study the people around you, and look out for people who might be watching or following you. Be aware of the local atmosphere: is it benign or hostile? Look out of the window before exiting a building or vehicle. As a matter of course, glance at the side mirrors of parked cars and at shop window reflections as you walk by.

If you see anyone suspicious around you, watching, following, or approaching you, make a mental note of his or her description and move away. If you find you are being followed, get into a place of safety such as a hotel, a large store with multiple exits, or a police station. Before making a move, criminals usually survey their prey to assess their worth and vulnerability; they will typically avoid following you into a secure or well-populated area where they would be more conspicuous and have a more difficult escape route.

Vigilance is your first line of defense against becoming another statistic in the war against crime. Being and looking alert and defensive will deter many thieves, while looking dazed, confused, lost, or sleepy, will attract them like a magnet.

At All Times

Travel with a partner if possible, and look out for each other. This will make your journey safer as well as more enjoyable.

Avoid standing out. Do not dress outrageously or in lavish clothes. Conversely, do not dress in jeans, sweats, or a tank top if the locals are wearing suits.

Refrain from ostentatious displays of wealth, such as wearing jewelry and costly watches. Expensive ornaments attract the attention of thieves.

Keep abreast of international news as well as events in the

country you are visiting. Read local newspapers and check the news on radio, TV, or Internet.

Stay alert, and be aware of your surroundings.

Watch out for anything suspicious, particularly unattended baggage in an airport, and report it to the authorities promptly.

Do not overindulge in alcohol. It impairs your ability to keep alert and makes you more of a target.

Show respect for the local culture. Be courteous, but not obsequious, to the locals; treat them as you would expect to be treated. Do not get into discussions about politics, race, or religion, as these could lead to arguments and unnecessary trouble. Be particularly careful not to disparage the local government, people, or way of life.

Never joke about hijacks, bombs, or terrorism. Other people might not share your sense of humor and you could find yourself under arrest due to a misunderstanding.

FLYING INTERNATIONALLY

Do not carry anything on board for anyone else, either by hand or in your checked luggage. Terrorists have been known to get a bomb onto a plane through the unwitting cooperation of a passenger they have befriended. Similarly, there are countless incidents of drugs being carried into a country by innocent passengers who have then been caught and apprehended upon arrival.

Never have anything in your check-in luggage that you cannot afford to lose, particularly sensitive personal or business information, personal effects, or valuables. Once it is checked in, your luggage is out of sight and beyond your control. There is always a chance it will be misdirected and arrive late, or that it will be ransacked and items stolen en route.

Discretion is a vital aspect of business confidentiality and personal security. Do not discuss your business plans, travel plans, personal details, personal wealth, or political or religious beliefs with or in front of other passengers, even if they are your acquaintances.

Be aware that your conversations are likely to be overheard, and your laptop screen seen, by others. Never conduct sensitive business on board a plane unless it is a private corporate jet. Airport business lounges are also a mine of business intelligence and therefore to be treated with caution.

Keep your conversations quiet. Americans have a reputation for being loud and insensitive, and stand out because of this. Keep use of in-flight telephones (and cell phones while the plane is on the ground) to a minimum.

Keep your carry-on bag under the seat in front of you where you can guard it, rather than in an overhead bin. If your bag is too big, remove your passport, laptop, and sensitive documents and keep them with you, while using an overhead bin in front of you for your bags. You cannot monitor an overhead bin behind you.

Abstain from alcohol and sleeping pills, so you can sleep lightly and be alert upon arrival.

ARRIVAL AT A FOREIGN AIRPORT

When you arrive at a foreign airport, be aware that you are no longer under U.S. jurisdiction. This might sound obvious, but some American travelers display an inflated sense of their own importance, which can irritate foreign officials. Go through Immigration and Customs efficiently with your passport and paperwork ready for inspection. Never argue with immigration or customs officials, even if you feel you are being harassed. In some countries these officials like to throw their weight around. If you are obliged to have any conversation with them, be pleasant and respectful, keeping it quiet and low key. Your objective is to get through the airport without drawing attention to yourself.

Keep your carry-on baggage close to hand, proceed promptly to the baggage area, and watch the designated carousel carefully for the arrival of your checked and clearly identifiable baggage — this is where baggage occasionally goes missing.

If you have a lot of luggage, or a heavy piece, it's best to take a trolley cart, if available, which will let you keep your luggage in sight, in front of you, and not overexert yourself. Keep your carry-on luggage secure by wedging it behind the heavier luggage or by strapping them together.

If you have a travel partner, keep close together and watch out for each other.

On exiting the Arrivals area, you may be accosted by solicitors wanting to carry your bags, arrange a taxi, offer you a ride to your hotel, and other enticing proposals. You will already have done your homework and know where you are going and how to get there. The car rental desk? Turn right out of the Arrivals hall. You also know a couple of phrases in the local language, or at least how to say no. Reject any solicitors firmly, do not engage them in conversation, and move on to the official porter, hotel shuttle desk, or rental car desk as appropriate. It is too easy for a criminal to offer to carry your briefcase, and then run off with it while you are still struggling with your outsize suitcase. If you need help with your luggage, use an official porter and have him handle the heavy stuff; then stick close to him. Keep anything vital in your carry-on, which should be in your hand or strapped to the heavy baggage so it cannot easily be seized when you get outside.

As mentioned previously, the favored method of transport in a medium-risk foreign country is to have a local friend or business colleague meet you with a car at the airport. Next best is to have a hotel limousine waiting for you. If a driver is meeting you and you do not know him by sight, be sure to check that he is indeed the appointed driver: use a prearranged password or phrase and ask to see his identification.

A taxi is the next option, but make sure it is an official taxi, with a meter and a taxi license. Never get into an unregistered or unofficial taxi, and never accept an offer to share a taxi with a stranger. Many overseas airports, conscious of security and taxi scams, have a separate taxi office in the Arrivals area, where you state your destination and pay in advance for the ride. This ensures that you do get an official taxi and pay the official rate. Other airports have a taxi dispatcher who just logs your name and destination and the registration number of the taxi when you get in. This at least provides the start of a trail for an investigator to follow if you go missing. If you have not paid in advance at the taxi office, find out from the driver approximately how much it will cost to get to your hotel before you accept a ride, and make sure he turns on the meter before you set off.

Hotel Security

Upon Arrival

Check that the entry lobby is secure. There should be at least a doorman and a receptionist covering the entrance. In addition, security personnel should be immediately on hand. In a high-risk city the security personnel should be armed. You can ask to speak to the manager or chief security officer if you are in doubt about security.

The questions you can ask in conducting your own security assessment include the policy for locking entrance doors by night, and whether the premises are covered by surveillance cameras, including the hallways, corridors, car park and rear entrances. Are the surveillance monitors watched twenty-four hours a day? You should also note whether hotel staff wear badges or carry ID and whether the hotel is well lit.

Merely provide your reservation number and credit card upon check-in. There is no need to state your name, nor should the reception person mention your name or room number aloud—if the receptionist announces your room number within earshot of others, get another room.

Take your map to the concierge and have him mark on it the key points, that is, the location of nearby police stations, hospitals, and the embassy or consulate, as well as the hotel itself. If you plan to visit your local office, other businesses, or tourist sites, mark these on your map at the same time.

Ask about any unsafe areas that you need to avoid, and circle them on the map so you won't stray into them.

If the local language and written script is unfamiliar to you, have the concierge write down the key points in the local language so you can show them to a local when asking directions. Write them down phonetically, too, so you can practice saying them yourself and be understood. Keep a hotel business card or piece of stationary with the address on it to show a policeman in case you get lost, particularly in a country that uses a different written language script.

Register your presence in country by calling or faxing the U.S. embassy or consulate, advising them of your name, company, hotel phone number, and any other contact numbers such as your cell phone. If you are traveling elsewhere in the country, provide a brief outline of your itinerary as well as your intended departure date. Take this opportunity to ask whether there is any unusual security situation to be aware of.

Room security

Have a member of the hotel staff show you to your room and, before they leave you there, check the room for safety before you accept it. If in doubt, ask for another room.

Refuse the lowest floors, which are most easily prone to burglary from outside, but also avoid rooms higher than the sixth floor, which can not be reached by fire ladders.

You need to check on keys and duplicates: if there are two keys, ask to hold the duplicate to avoid someone else checking it out and entering your room. Electronic keys are preferable to manual keys, as they are more secure and can be quickly canceled or changed, but they are not yet universal. Note whether the room doors double-lock. If so, double-lock the door every time you leave the room to engage the additional bolts.

You also need to check on locking the room from inside, on whether the door mechanism locks with dead bolts into the door frame, on whether there is a stout door chain, and whether the peephole works properly.

Confirm how the windows and any other entrances such as French doors or interconnecting doors are secured.

Avoid taking a room with an interconnecting door to another room, unless that room is to be occupied by a traveling associate of yours. For similar reasons, check carefully if there is a balcony, to see whether someone could get to it from outside and break into your room unobserved.

If there is a wall safe in the room, check to see how secure it is. It should be bolted into the wall from inside the safe so that the whole thing cannot be stolen. If it has a manual key lock, ask about other keys — a manual-locking room safe is unlikely to be secure, as a previous guest or hotel worker may have made a duplicate key. A combination-lock system is more secure, provided you set a new combination, and assuming the safe has a dead-bolt mechanism. If there is no room safe, or you are unsure that it is adequate, ask about a hotel safety deposit box. Such a box should be for your exclusive use, and should have a two-key opening system so that both your key and the manager's key are needed together to open the safe. As soon as you have a secure safe or safety deposit box arranged, use it to store your excess cash, traveler's checks, airline tickets, and valuables.

Fire Precautions

Fire is always a risk in a hotel. There should be a smoke detector and sprinkler system in your room and in the hallways and public rooms. Upon arrival you must verify the proximity to your room of the nearest fire escapes, fire-fighting equipment, and house phones.

Plan your emergency evacuation procedure and routes. Study the fire exits and make sure you know how to get to them from your room in dark and smoke conditions — not just the nearest one but the alternates, too. Know where the nearest fire extinguisher and hose reel is. Make sure the fire exits and stairways are not blocked up or locked, either on your floor or at the street level. At the same time make sure the fire exit is locked to outside access.

When you retire, keep a set of clothes and shoes by the bed with a flashlight, ready for an emergency exit. Make sure you can locate the flashlight quickly in the dark; it will be the first thing you need. As a bedtime routine, consider keeping it in one of your shoes beside the bed. Keep your room keys, car keys, cell phone, wallet, and passport in a grab bag or money belt by the bed as well.

Read the section below entitled "In Case of a Hotel Fire."

Hotel Routine

Do not enter your room in the dark. Leave a light and the TV or radio on in the room when you go out. Do not use the Please Make up Room sign; it is an obvious signal that the room is taken and is most likely unoccupied.

Do not hang your breakfast order, laundry, or other service request outside your door. It is an invitation for a criminal impersonating a hotel service person to knock on your door at breakfast time and gain entry into your room. It also tells a criminal how many people are occupying the room, and at least one of their names. If you want to avail yourself of room service meals or other services, just call in the order when you want it. After eating a meal in your room, place the tray in the corridor well away from your own door. What you have eaten can also indicate the number and type of people occupying a room.

Secure all windows and patio doors before you leave your room, and every time you return, confirm that the room is empty and that the windows and doors are still secure. A hotel employee could have been in the room in your absence and have left a window open or unlocked either by mistake or to assist a thief. Never enter your room if the door is open or unlocked. Get hotel security to go in first.

Make it a habit to check your room every time you enter. Prop the door open and quickly scan every room and closet, including the shower and under the bed, to make sure you are alone. Start with the nearest hiding places and work your way in, keeping your escape route to the corridor open. Carry out this procedure quickly, then go and lock your door.

Do not open the door to a caller without identifying the visitor first through the closed door and peephole, even if it is a supposed hotel employee. If a hotel employee or maintenance worker asks to enter your room unexpectedly, call the management to verify their identity and reason for being there before letting them in. Use the peephole first and open the door on the door chain once you are satisfied, but remember that a person in a uniform jacket, or even a child, may be used as a ploy to get you to open your door.

If you have a flimsy door or lock, use a door jam or a chair to jam the door when you go to bed. Do not rely on the lock and door chain. With a manual lock, once inside your room, keep the door locked, leaving the key turned inside the lock so that someone outside cannot easily push it through.

Do not divulge your room number even for business reasons, except to your trusted travel partner. Let people call you by going through the hotel operator (who should connect callers without divulging your room number), and do not state your name or room number when answering the phone. Meet visitors in the lobby, not in your room.

Leave valuables in the room safe, the hotel safe, or out of sight on your person. Better yet, leave them at home. Do not attempt to hide anything in a hotel room — thieves know all the best hiding places!

Do not leave personal information in your room, including

your travel itinerary, and do not discard personal or business documents in your room's trash bin.

Hotel Public Areas

Avoid idle chatter with strangers and be suspicious of pickups. Hotel bars and foyers are favorite preying grounds for confidence tricksters and thieves. Glamorous prostitutes are often used as bait to trap unwary businessmen. The dangers of letting an unknown person into your room cannot be overstated. Apart from the immediate threats of theft, blackmail, and extortion, there is the real danger that a prostitute, acting as part of a gang, will let an accomplice into your room and that you will be assaulted and robbed.

Do not get into an elevator alone with anyone who looks in the least shady. Get out immediately if you are alone and someone suspicious gets in. Conversely, beware of pickpockets in a crowded elevator. Let other people press their floor buttons before you, and be wary of anyone else getting out on your floor. If you are followed when you get out of the elevator, step back inside the elevator before the door closes. Report any suspicious encounters or activities to hotel security staff.

Protect your privacy and room information carefully. When you sign your name and room number on a dining bill or bar tab, turn it face down and make sure the waiter picks it up before you leave the table or bar. Do not state your name unnecessarily or mention your room number loudly when asking for your messages at the reception desk.

Do not hand out business cards unnecessarily, or display a business label on your briefcase. You do not want everyone to know that you are the head of International Widgets and therefore worth a fortune in ransom. Similarly, if attending a convention, remove your identity badge before leaving the convention area.

Do not display your room key if it has a number tag on it. Some hotels attach a large, room-numbered tag to their keys to dissuade guests from removing the key from the property. You should never display such a tag, and you should not be persuaded by this tactic to leave your key at reception when you go out; it's a sure sign that your room is unoccupied. Rather, remove the tag and leave that in your room, keeping just the key on your person when you go out.

Steer clear of public restrooms. Use the restroom in your own hotel room when possible, or use one in another hotel or a restaurant as second best (where there is no fast exit to the street for an attacker). If you do have to use a public restroom, select one that several other people are using and stay close to the exit. People are particularly vulnerable to assault in restrooms, so do not linger. Men are more vulnerable while using the urinal, as someone can approach from behind and attack. Use a stall, and lock the door for safety. Keep your briefcase or purse where it cannot be snatched under or over the door or walls. Do not put your hand near the floor to pick something up; you could be grabbed from the next-door stall.

Be especially vigilant in the hotel car park. Do not approach your car unless it is clear of strangers all around, and do not enter your car without first checking that it is unoccupied. Have your keys ready so you can get immediately into your car, lock the doors, and start the engine. Use the horn or remote alarm if you feel threatened.

Conversely, when parking in a hotel car park, make sure you

know the way into the hotel before you park. Park close to the entrance in a well-lit area. Even in daylight, park under a lamp or surveillance camera. Leave your car swiftly, being sure to lock it, and move into the hotel. If you see anything suspicious or troubling, including an absence of activity, drive to the front entrance and have the valet park your car, or get an escort into the car park and back into the hotel.

If you have baggage or shopping to take into the hotel, drive up to the entrance and entrust it to the concierge. Then, when you park your car, you will not be carrying something worth stealing, will have both hands free to protect yourself, and, being unencumbered with baggage, will be better able to take evasive action if a threat materializes.

Street Smarts

Vigilance is the key to personal safety. Try to maintain "all-round vision," that is, a sense of what is happening around you at all times. It may ensure your safety and even save your life. The following points summarize the basic precautions you should take abroad while walking around or traveling outside your hotel.

The way you dress is an important aspect of your security precautions. Dress modestly in order to blend in. Do not wear jewelry, an expensive-looking watch (even a fake), or carry an expensive-looking bag, all of which will set you up as a potential target. Leave the college ring and the Gucci bag at home and wear an inexpensive watch. Do not wear shorts unless it is accepted practice among the locals. Wear sensible shoes that you can walk or run in.

Steer clear of American brand-name restaurants as well as popular bars and nightclubs frequented by Western tourists. They tend to attract criminals, and also make attractive targets for terrorists.

Where possible, travel with a friend or colleague. An accompanied person is less likely to be assaulted than someone who is alone. In addition, two people together can protect themselves far better than one alone.

If you are walking with a partner or in a group, have an agreed-upon rendezvous plan in case you become unintentionally separated. This can be as simple as arranging to meet back at a certain restaurant on the hour. You can update your rendezvous plan or meeting point frequently while you move around, as long as you are in contact, so that it's not too far to go back to if you get separated. Avoid designating a rendezvous point where the first person there is obliged to loiter outside looking lost. Of course, if you have cell phones you can use those, or you can call each other's hotel voice mail to report your location and intentions. The important thing is to have a lost-contact plan and to make sure everyone knows what it is.

Keep abreast of current local politics through daily news reports. Changes in the local political situation, or even a situation involving the USA in a different country, may have an impact on local feelings, which could be expressed in anti-American sentiment and street hostility. Listen to U.S. news stations or the BBC World Service on short-wave radio or via the Internet to stay informed.

Keep your politics and your views on cultural differences to yourself and behave respectfully, particularly when visiting religious sites or rural communities. Cultural awareness and conformity is not only a safety precaution, but is very good business and social practice and will make your trip a lot more pleasant.

Avoid routine, such as a daily nine a.m. visit to the local office.

Vary your time, routine, and route so your schedule is not predictable to a criminal. If you are staying for more than a week in a high-risk area, consider changing your hotel every few days.

Do not go jogging outside the hotel; this marks you as an American and therefore a target. Although you might not be carrying anything valuable, you are vulnerable to assault or kidnap when jogging. Keep fit and stay safe by using the exercise facilities inside the hotel.

If you are walking alone, try to stick close to another couple or group. When walking, keep to the inside of the sidewalk, away from the road, but without passing too close to doorways or corners of buildings where someone could be hiding to accost you. You should walk facing the oncoming traffic, to prevent a car creeping up from behind. Do not wander off the beaten track; stick to main pedestrian routes and well-lighted areas, avoiding shortcuts and empty side streets.

Look up and look confident. Look around but avoid prolonged eye contact—you do not want to look threatening, but you certainly don't want to look inviting!

If you are carrying a briefcase in public, keep it on the inside, away from the street, and keep your spare hand free. If walking in pairs, keep bags or briefcases between the two of you. A lady should carry her purse strapped across her body, and hanging to the inside if walking with a partner. In high-risk areas it is best to leave the briefcase and purse behind and keep your effects in a zipped or Velcro-fastened inside jacket pocket, supplemented by a concealed money belt. This makes life hard for a pickpocket, there is nothing a thief can notice and grab, and you have both hands free.

Before shopping, plan how you are going to get your purchases back to your hotel. If you are driving yourself, park close to the store to avoid carrying too much and having both hands full when walking. Put your shopping straight into your car, or send it directly back to your hotel, rather than carrying it farther than necessary. If purchasing an expensive item, arrange for it to be taken to your hotel and delivered to the concierge to hold for you. You can pay for it on delivery (but again, remember not to give out your room number).

When using a credit card, keep it in your sight so it cannot be copied, and make sure it is swiped only once for your purchase. Then, be sure to read the invoice details carefully before you sign, taking care to verify that you have the correct receipt and are handed back the correct card. Never leave a credit card behind a bar to run up a tab; by the time you are ready to leave, it could be clear across town, with thousands of additional dollars chalked up to your account.

The easiest targets for pickpockets are people standing still or sitting down. If you are not moving, a pickpocket or thief has time to size you up, plan an assault, and wait for a perfect moment when no one else is watching. Keep moving if you can, but if you must stand still, keep your back to a wall and be alert.

Stay away from isolated locations, particularly beaches and unfrequented areas of parks. You are vulnerable in any isolated location, and there is likely to be no help close at hand.

Minimize your night time travel. Darkness is the preferred cover for robbers to strike because it aids concealment and surprise and it reduces the chance of recognition and subsequent identification. If you are out after dark, stick to populated areas that are well lighted.

Stay away from crowds, political gatherings, and demonstrations, even if you sympathize with the cause. Such crowds, with attendant jostling, distractions, and noise, are a gold mine for pickpockets. Remember that demonstrations—particularly antigovernment demonstrations—and sporting events in foreign countries can get rough quickly, and that the police may respond robustly and indiscriminately with water cannon, batons, and live bullets. If you find yourself caught up in a demonstration or other unruly gathering, work your way to the edge of the crowd, then move indoors into a place of safety such as a store or hotel.

Be alert for pickpockets, street gangs, and possible bag snatchers on foot or on motorbikes. If you see anything suspicious coming toward you, move away, enter a store, or cross the street.

Look out for people who appear out of place, trying to shield their features and hide their identity, for instance, or concealing what could be a weapon under a coat.

Keep alert for people watching or following you; they could be trying to set you up for robbery or kidnap. Use reflections in shop windows or car wing mirrors to monitor your rear. If you think you are being followed, you can check by entering a store and then leaving by a different exit, or getting on a bus and then off again after a couple of stops. If you have confirmed that you are being followed, get into a place of safety as quickly as possible.

If someone accosts you to ask questions or directions, be wary and keep your distance. Do not bend down close to answer questions from a person in a car—you could be robbed, or bundled into the car by a third party.

Do not get involved in street surveys, requests for assistance, or conversations with strangers, even if they are just asking the time; there is frequently a setup or scam involved. Be suspicious and wary when approached. If accosted, use your command of the local language to say no, and move away. Never accept food, drink, or even gum from strangers—it may be drugged.

If someone grabs your arm, jostles you, wants to help wipe something from your jacket, or otherwise tries to distract you, shout, shake them off, and break away. Pickpockets commonly work in pairs and frequently use an accomplice, possibly a woman or child, to distract their target.

If you want to take photographs, you should restrict this to tourist areas. Photography often marks you as a tourist, anyway, so take your photo, put away your camera, and move on. As always, it's important to be aware of your surroundings and not get immersed in setting up the perfect shot while your pocket is being picked.

Do not take close-up photographs of strangers, particularly women, without their permission. In many countries it is considered extremely offensive and can lead to a hostile confrontation.

Do not take photographs of uniformed personnel or military equipment without permission from an official. Never take photographs on or near military installations: you may be accused of spying. Some English nationals were recently arrested and tried for espionage in Greece, a NATO ally, after taking photographs outside an airbase.

Unless you are a politician being paid to speak, keep your political views to yourself. If asked for an opinion on some aspect of U.S. foreign policy, for example, it's better to declare ignorance than to state a position and invite hostility.

Leave most of your money, your passport, tickets, and any extra credit cards in the hotel safe, and carry with you just enough for the day, keeping this money and one credit card in an inside pocket or preferably in a concealed money belt. Carry an old wallet with a little money and even an expired credit card, which you can use or lose and not be concerned about. In the event that your pocket is picked, or you are robbed or held up, you can give up the old wallet and be grateful that you have survived unscathed.

Do not be tempted to change your dollars into local currency on the black market, even if the rate is much better than the official one. Street transactions are fraught with danger; you could be robbed before, during or afterward, you could be cheated with counterfeit money, you could be blackmailed, or be caught by the authorities and charged with a currency offense.

Do not carry anything in your briefcase or bag that you cannot afford to lose. Business papers and computer files must be duplicated and backed up elsewhere. Personal details such as bank accounts and passwords should not be carried around. Keep passports and credit cards hidden away in a money belt while keeping just a little money in your wallet.

Avoid using your cell phone in public. You are very vulnerable while distracted on a telephone, your conversation is likely to be overheard, and your cell phone itself could get snatched. If you have to use your cell phone, or a pay phone, keep your conversation brief, keep your back to the wall, and be extra alert.

Do not discuss your business plans, travel plans, personal details, personal wealth, or political or religious beliefs with strangers or within earshot of strangers. Be sensitive to eavesdroppers.

If planning to attend a theater or other entertainment event, get your tickets in advance over the Internet or from your hotel. Your standing in line for tickets offers ticket scalpers and pickpockets an opportunity to accost you.

If you feel threatened on the street, get into a store, restaurant, or busy public area. Call the police or ask for assistance from store security before venturing back onto the street.

If, despite all precautions, you do get robbed, notify the police immediately and then call to cancel any lost credit cards and documents. This means calling credit-card companies, the airline ticket office, and, if you lost your passport, the consulate.

Be Proactive

Foiling terrorist plans or casual crime is not just up to the police and intelligence services. The public, especially the traveling public, can and does make a significant contribution. If you see a suspicious event or witness a crime, make an immediate mental note of details and descriptions, write it down before you forget some vital element, and report the incident promptly to the police, the airline, or appropriate security authorities.

Banks and Automatic Teller Machines

Before arriving in a foreign country, get some local currency—at least enough for your first couple of days in country—in low value bills, including small denominations for tips.

Carry traveler's checks or a credit card rather than a lot of cash. In the case of traveler's checks, make sure you sign them before leaving home and that a record of the serial numbers is in your possession and a copy at home or in your office.

Always avoid using ATMs unless they are in a secure place. Change money or use the ATM inside a bank if possible. Put away your money before leaving the bank. If using an external ATM, look around and make sure you are not being watched and that no one is too close. If uncertain, move away and find another ATM. Shield the keypad when entering your PIN number. Thieves use long-range cameras and other methods to copy

PIN numbers. Have a partner wait nearby, watching you from the car and ready to alert you to trouble, or standing behind you and looking outward.

While using the cash dispenser at a drive-in ATM, keep your doors locked, car in gear, and foot on the brake, ready to drive away. Keep an eye on the mirrors to watch for anyone creeping up alongside the car to rob you. If you are threatened, abandon your card and drive away without your cash.

Using an ATM immediately classifies you as someone in possession of money and therefore a target. Be extra vigilant, after coming out of a bank or when leaving an ATM, for followers and muggers. The ATM itself may have photo surveillance, but the area beyond it is probably not monitored.

LOCAL TRANSPORTATION

Appropriate Secure Transport

Use appropriate transport to meet the threat. Visitors to London, for instance, should be happy with the black taxis. The London subway, known there as "the Tube," and the buses, are generally safe also. On the other hand, many countries do not have a safe taxi or public transport system. Your research and preparation will lead you to decide what is secure and appropriate in each case. If you are the average businessman or tourist, the most secure form of transport you are likely to need is to have a trusted local business partner or associate pick you up from the hotel and provide all your transportation needs. At the other end of the spectrum, in a high-risk area, an armor-protected vehicle should be used, with a trusted driver trained in defensive driving techniques. The advice that follows should be taken in the context of the local situation based on the research you have done about the country. Some of the precautions may be excessive in the safer countries; only you can decide what is appropriate. Just remember the old maxim: "It is better to be safe than sorry."

Hotel Limousine

Where possible, use hotel limousines or shuttles rather than taxis. They are safer because the driver is normally a registered contractor or employee of the hotel.

There is no need to state your destination when reserving a limousine. Tell the driver at the last minute where you want to go. Do not discuss your business or personal plans with the driver, on the phone, or with your partner, while you are in the vehicle.

If you go to a meeting, have the limousine wait, or arrange in advance for it to return to pick you up afterward.

Taxis

If you must use a taxi, use only an official, licensed cab, make sure your hotel concierge arranges it, knows where you are going, advises you how much it should cost, and makes a note of the license number. Keep the phone number of this official cab company, so you can call to have them collect you later if necessary.

To avoid a situation where you have to take a taxi off the street, use the phone to call the approved cab company, or make appropriate arrangements in advance for your return.

Your map study will tell you if you are being driven directly to the place you want to get to. If you are in a taxi and it seems to be going off course, bail out at the earliest opportunity and get into a place of safety. Make a mental note of safe spots in the area as you travel, and learn how to get back to them. In addition to friendly embassies and consulates, you should already be aware of the locations of police stations, hospitals, and other hotels, and have them marked on your map.

Driving Yourself

If you intend to drive yourself, rent from a reputable international agency with reliable cars, and make sure you have appropriate accident insurance. Avoid renting an ostentatious car, but get one with plenty of power and central locking, and that is not labeled as a rental.

Have the car delivered to your hotel, if possible, rather than collecting it from the airport upon arrival, especially if you are arriving after dark.

When taking a car from the airport, make sure you study the local map that gets you out of the airport, as well as the route map to your destination. Do this before you leave the rental company office. The rental company should give you clear directions for the first part. Getting lost as you exit an airport marks you as a stranger and sets you up as a target.

Make sure you are familiar with local road signs and traffic regulations before you set out. Sign symbols may differ from the U.S. conventions—notices and road signs might not even be in English!

Make sure your emergency contact list includes the car-rental office's local phone number, the emergency roadside assistance contact number, and your reservation number.

Check that a spare tire, jack, and wrench are provided. Before driving off, familiarize yourself with all of the car's features and controls; make sure they all work, and check to see that the gas tank is full. Drive the car around the block as soon as you collect it from the rental agency to check the steering, lights, brakes, and power. Take it straight back if anything doesn't work properly.

Keep all personal property, maps, and documents out of sight in the glove compartment or locked in the trunk, whether you are driving or parked. Conceal any material that identifies your car as a rental, including the rental contract and rental company maps and stickers, because a rental car is a magnet for thieves.

If you have to stop to check the map, do so outside a police station or other safe spot. Do not stop along a deserted road to look at your map, especially at night.

Make sure you are alone or unobserved before you open the trunk, then do your business and close it as quickly as possible. Do not leave your car unattended after putting things in the trunk; drive away, even if only to another parking space in a different area, before leaving the car.

In built-up areas, always drive with windows closed and doors locked. Never, under any circumstances, drive with an open window and an arm resting on the window ledge. Your watch could get snatched, or you could be attacked, at a stop. Air conditioning is, for this reason, a desirable feature on a rental.

Do not place any valuable item on the passenger seat; it invites a smash-and-grab assault. Briefcases and purses should go under the seat or in the locked trunk.

Keep a close eye on the rearview mirror and watch out for anyone following you. If you are being followed, get to a crowded public area, a large hotel, or a police station for safety. Do not lead a follower to your destination if it is your own hotel or office.

Avoid driving at night if possible, particularly in high-threat areas. Plan your trips so you depart in daylight and arrive at your destination before dark.

Plan ahead to identify and minimize possible choke points where you will be stationary and therefore vulnerable. Where traffic is stopped ahead of you at a traffic signal, slow down your approach and try to time your arrival at the signal as the traffic moves on. At stops, keep a distance from the car in front so you can maneuver around it quickly in an emergency. In some cities in South America, smash-and-grab raids have become quite commonplace at traffic lights.

If someone tries to get into your car or smash a window at a traffic stop, drive forward and back continuously between the cars ahead and behind to prevent it. Even if it's only a short distance, such movements can be effective in breaking up an attack. Use your horn at the same time. Drive around the car ahead if the route beyond is clear, even if you have to drive on the sidewalk. If you are at a stoplight, drive on or turn the corner, even if the light is red, to escape an attack.

When stopping or parking, choose a well-lighted, well-populated place with good all-round vision. Park close to shops in an open car park. Select a manned car park rather than an automatic one, and park near the attendant if possible. Remember when parking in daylight that it may be dark when you return, so park under a streetlight. In multistory car parks, use spaces where there are several other people in sight.

When you park, look around before exiting the car. Look for suspicious people loitering or watching. If in doubt, drive off and go elsewhere.

In a car park, reverse into your chosen space so you can drive away quickly. After parking, leave your car swiftly, being sure to lock it, and move away.

When you return to your parked car, look around carefully before approaching. If anyone is loitering nearby, do not approach your car until they have left, or go and fetch a security guard or policeman. When you get to your car, check quickly for any signs of tampering, look underneath for any suspicious objects, and check that no one is already inside. If there has been any tampering, or if you see anything suspicious, do not open the car but move away immediately and get help. Have your keys ready so that, if everything is fine, you can get into your car quickly, lock the doors, and drive away. Do not linger in your car in the car park. If you feel threatened, sound the horn or remote alarm, if necessary, to attract attention.

At the hotel or restaurant, use the valet parking, especially at night, to avoid walking around a car park. Make sure that it's a genuine valet, though, and that you're not just donating your car to a local private charity. Obviously, you do not leave any valuables in the car, and hand over only the door and ignition keys.

Do not be tempted to park illegally on the assumption that a parking ticket in London, say, will not catch up with you in the USA. If you return to find your car has been towed or clamped, and have to start walking, you will be immediately vulnerable.

Keep the gas tank filled and do not begin a long journey without knowing where you can refill. Running out of gas can be a dangerous mistake. In a gas station, keep the car locked while you go to pay.

In case of a breakdown, your first priority should be to get to a safe place. Try to get there in the car if it isn't totally immobilized. If you decide to abandon it, get the car off the road and lock it, taking anything vital with you, and get yourself to the nearest safe place. With any luck this will be a public building, such as a nearby restaurant, from where you can see your car. Use your cell phone to call for assistance. Do not sit looking helpless by a broken-down car. If there is no safe place nearby, stay in your car with the doors locked, and, if you have been unable to call for assistance, use your lights and horn to attract attention.

Do not fall for the well-used ploy of criminals who will wave at you and indicate, in an effort to get you to pull over, that there is something wrong with your car. Another ploy is to bump your car to simulate an accident and make you pull over, before robbing you or stealing the car.

Drinking and driving is the number one cause of accidents to businessmen overseas. If you add drink to the other difficulties of driving abroad—an unfamiliar car, unknown roads, and different driving conditions—it's easy to understand why this is so. Don't drink and drive.

If the police stop you in a non-English-speaking country, produce your International Driving Permit first. It has the advantage of being written in several languages. Note that you might have to produce your regular driver's license as well. Some countries allow the police the right to levy on-the-spot fines for speeding. Although this is well regulated in Europe, for instance, it is a system open to corruption in other parts of the world. If you are in one of the latter countries, keep your wealth out of sight and display only your spare wallet, the one with $30 in it.

Trains and Subways

Trains and subways vary considerably in risk from one city to another, from one part of the track to another, and from one time of day to another. Take local advice before traveling by train or subway, and avoid subways at night.

♦ Travel with a partner if possible. In any case, avoid traveling in a carriage on your own. There is usually safety in numbers.

♦ Choose a carriage near to the conductor or guard if there is one.

♦ Do not sleep in a public compartment on a train unless your partner is awake to guard you and your belongings. If traveling in a sleeper compartment on a train, lock or jam your door.

♦ If you feel uncomfortable or intimidated in a carriage, get off at the next stop or get up and change carriages.

Buses

Treat buses, like trains, with caution, and use them only in countries where hijack and open banditry are unknown.

You need to be alert on a bus to protect yourself from criminals.

Travel with a partner if possible and do not both sleep simultaneously. At a stop, do not both get off the bus unless you take your baggage with you or everyone is off and the bus is verifiably locked and guarded.

If you are traveling with baggage inside the bus, keep it in view or under your feet. If it's in an overhead bin it could be easily rifled. Sneaky robbers have been known to cut into bags and remove the contents without moving the bag or disturbing the owner. If that's a risk where you are going, lining your bag with chicken wire may foil this move.

Light Aircraft

For convenience and safety, taking a local flight by light or commuter aircraft may be a sensible alternative to driving, though it is said that 75 percent of aircraft accidents happen in countries that account for only 12 percent of all air traffic. Naturally, you will want to check the safety record of the company you choose to fly with before committing yourself. Aircraft maintenance in certain Third World countries is not as diligent as it might be. Spare parts are often in short supply, money is tight, and maintenance training is poor. Wary travelers prefer twin-engine planes in these places.

Be sure that your flight plan skirts around any hostile territory if there is an insurgency going on; you don't want to survive a forced landing only to be kidnapped by local bandits.

HEALTH WHILE TRAVELING

In tropical countries, many visitors fall victim to the heat and to diarrhea and similar illnesses caused by eating and drinking contaminated foods and beverages. Only eat recently prepared food that has been thoroughly cooked and is still hot. Drink plenty of bottled water or bottled drinks to prevent dehydration. Wash your hands frequently with soap and water.

If you succumb to diarrhea, keep drinking plenty of clean bottled water to avoid dehydration, and keep eating.

In tropical climates, avoid salads, raw vegetables, cold meat, and shellfish. Do not eat food that has been left uncovered; any food that has flies on it will probably make you ill. If you buy your own fruit and vegetables from a market, wash them carefully in purified water or peel them before eating.

Do not drink tap water or put ice made from tap water in your drinks unless you are certain the water is safe. Contaminated water-borne diseases include Hepatitis A and typhoid fever. If you are in an area where bottled water or drinks are not available, use a water-purification system, filter your water and add purification tablets, and boil it before drinking.

Sunburn and heat exhaustion are common ailments for business people in warm foreign countries, particularly for people used to living indoors and working in air-conditioned environments. Apply sunscreen to avoid the first. Wear a hat and loose clothes, drink plenty of fluids, and exercise cautiously to prevent the second.

Mosquitoes carry diseases such as malaria (which can be fatal). Take your anti-malarial precautions conscientiously; stay away from areas of fetid groundwater, take regular anti-malarial pills, use mosquito repellent, and keep yourself covered up as much as possible between dusk and dawn, when mosquitoes are most active. If you become unwell after being in a malarial area, with fever, diarrhea and joint pains, get immediate medical attention. Have your blood tested for malaria even if your illness starts several weeks after you return home.

Do not go about barefoot. It exposes you to cuts and scrapes as well as parasites. In tropical areas, cuts and scrapes can quickly become infected. Treat even the smallest cut seriously: clean it immediately and apply antiseptic ointment. Antibiotics may be needed if infection sets in.

Get local advice before swimming in the sea. Ask about dangerous fish, jellyfish, or sand insects. Untreated sewage is frequently a health hazard near populated areas. Cuts and scrapes from coral reefs are particularly quick to become infected. See a doctor if you cut yourself on coral, but avoid the problem in the first place by wearing athletic shoes while walking or swimming near a reef.

Do not swim in tropical rivers and lakes without getting competent local advice. Waterborne diseases abound in Africa and Asia. Bilharzia can be contracted from even a splash of contaminated water on the skin. It is usually best to confine your swimming to chlorinated swimming pools.

Animal bites are another serious problem. If you are in a rabies-infested country (or if you are uncertain) and get bitten, wash the wound thoroughly and seek immediate medical attention, even for a minor bite. Rabies is not confined to dogs; it can be carried by other animals such as the vampire bat, and even by birds. Additionally, rabies can be contracted without biting if an animal licks an existing scratch or your open skin. Tourists have caught rabies while feeding monkeys. In addition to immediate medical attention, report any such animal-contact incident to your doctor immediately upon returning home, even if you have been treated abroad.

Unprotected sex with strangers is a major health risk. Abstinence is the first line of defense; failing that, always use a condom.

HIV or the AIDS virus is widespread in many parts of the world, particularly Africa. Blood supplies and needles may be tainted. You cannot carry a spare blood supply, but you should take your own clean syringe and needles in your first-aid pack, in case emergency treatment requires injections or taking blood samples. If you're traveling with a partner or a group, it's a good idea to know everyone's blood type should one of you require a blood transfusion and need a donor.

DEPARTURE FROM A FOREIGN COUNTRY

When preparing to leave, be sure to plan your departure carefully, particularly your secure mode of transport to the airport.

Plan to get a daytime or early evening flight so you arrive at your departure airport in daylight.

Be careful to allow plenty of time, whether you're using the services of a trusted local friend or business colleague to get to the airport, or taking the hotel limousine. Accidents, as well as robberies, happen when people get rushed and forget about safety. Do not relax your vigilance on the way to the airport. Whether taking a limousine, taxi, or other car, stow all your baggage in the trunk before setting off, and make sure the trunk is locked.

Incidentally, do not be tempted to overstay your visa duration, however much you are enjoying your visit or however lucrative the long-awaited business opportunity. A visa can usually be extended in country before it expires, but an expired visa can lead to a fine or imprisonment.

Before leaving your hotel, repack your baggage to be sure there is nothing in it that you do not know about, then lock it and keep it under your control all the way to the airport. Do not agree to take anything with you for someone else, either in your carry-on or check-in baggage, even if it's a last-minute gift or memento.

Keep firm control of your baggage at the airport. Be particularly cautious in the departure area, and while you're talking at the check-in desk, to ensure that your baggage is guarded continuously, as well as locked. A drug trafficker, smuggler, or terrorist agent may seek an opportunity to slip something into your bags. Do not ask a stranger to watch your bags, nor agree to watch anyone else's for any reason. At the check-in desk, keep your carry-on bag or briefcase on the counter in front of you or firmly under your foot.

Before leaving the check-in desk, make sure your tickets are in order and that all onward ticket segments are still together in your ticket folder—sometimes things slip out! Do not loiter in the public area or remain longer than necessary at the check-in facility, but get through the security check and into the departure area. The departure area is more secure, since everyone, in theory, will have passed through the security check.

It's important to be vigilant and proactive in any airport. If you see unattended baggage, a suspicious-looking package being dropped into a trash can, or someone tampering with another passenger's luggage, move apart and immediately notify someone in authority.

When passing through the security check and baggage X-ray facility, keep a close eye on your personal effects as they go through the scanner. Do not put them on the conveyor belt until your way through is clear; in a busy airport, it's a common trick for a thief to delay you at the X-ray scanner while your bag or laptop is stolen by his accomplice who has already passed through the checkpoint.

Once on the plane, you might be tempted to breathe a sigh of relief and to start reviewing with your neighboring passenger the shortcomings of the country you are leaving. Do not do this. As a certain British passenger on a flight out of the Middle East will recall, if the plane is diverted back to the departure area, and your neighbor turns out to be that country's chief of secret police, you may get marched off the plane and into serious trouble.

Remember that your journey does not end until you are safely back in your house. Airports in the USA are also a haven for thieves watching out for sleep-deprived and careless victims emerging from the international Arrivals area. Keep your guard up until you get home.

Even after you are safely home from an overseas trip you must monitor your health for several weeks. If you develop any sickness, let your doctor know the symptoms, where you have been, and what precautions you took or failed to take. Some diseases, such as malaria, can manifest themselves weeks after exposure.

Miscellaneous Notes

Laptop Computers

Laptops and Personal Digital Assistants (PDAs) are routinely stolen, particularly from hotel conference rooms. Unless you really need it on your trip, leave your laptop at home. Consider using the facilities of your local office, such as their office computers and data network, if you are on a business trip. Use an Internet café if you're on vacation and merely want to check your e-mail.

Never leave your laptop unattended unless it is locked up. Apart from locking it in the hotel safe there are many locking and alarm systems on the market. These vary from a steel cable and lock, which allow you to secure your laptop to a bed frame or other encumbrance, to a motion-detector alarm, which sounds if someone moves the laptop.

Make sure you carry only the minimum needed data on your laptop, not your company's entire finances, product development plans, and business plan. Make sure that the data you do carry is securely backed up elsewhere.

Do not carry personal data on your laptop. Encrypt sensitive business data—but beware of laws regarding export of sophisticated encryption technology from the USA, and laws in some countries banning encryption!

Consider keeping your encrypted data on a removable drive or memory card, which you can lock up separately or carry securely on your person.

Set your encryption program to be activated every time you shut down or close the lid on your laptop or PDA, or whenever it's inactive for more than a few minutes. That way, even if it does get stolen, the data on it will be well protected.

Make an emergency plan in case the worst happens and your laptop does get stolen. Hopefully, for instance, you still have your local contact list on paper.

When you take your laptop through an airport security check, you may be asked to switch it on, so make sure you have a charged battery available.

Notes for Women

Women face additional problems, particularly when traveling alone. Women will often find that their treatment overseas differs from what they expect in the USA. Depending on the country, the local women might be treated as second-class citizens, expected to defer to men at all times, or might be dismissed as mere sex objects. To avoid any unpleasant surprises, check the role and customs of women in the society you plan to visit.

If you travel alone, ladies, be prepared for some sexual harassment, particularly in foreign countries where it might not even be considered harassment, and be prepared to deal with it firmly. It could be a short step from harassment to sexual assault. Avoid the inevitable pickup attempt by discouraging attention in the first place. This can be done by not sitting alone next to a spare seat or standing alone looking lost, and by not looking alluring or available.

Most women are aware of the risk of assault and rape, and that the risks of both are increased by being alone. Try to look attached, or part of a group, even if you are not. Two women traveling together will be at less risk than one alone, and to avoid unwanted attention can look attached by walking arm in arm.

Jewelry should be left at home, as previously noted, but you might want to wear a simple wedding band to help discourage advances. To avoid unwelcome attention, one blonde lady of my acquaintance wears a black wig when traveling in Asia and the Middle East, on the basis that most local women there have dark hair.

Most of the advice in other sections of this Manual applies even more urgently to women. Wear sensible shoes, not high heels, dress modestly, and use makeup sparingly. Make sure you know the local word for "No", and be prepared to use it loudly and forcefully to deter unwanted attention. If you feel uncomfortable somewhere, then move away.

If traveling unaccompanied, but as part of a group, stick to the group activities rather than going off alone.

When driving a car, follow the precautions already outlined, and be sure to hide your purse, camera, and any other attractive items under the seat, not on the passenger or rear seat.

In the hotel, ask for a room next to another group member or acquaintance, so help is close by. If you use room service, pay attention to the earlier comments about placing the used tray well away from your room. Do not leave it inside your room for the cleaning service to deal with; often, they will just put it outside your door, where lipstick or some other indicator may give away the presence of a woman, while the number of plates and utensils could indicate that you are alone.

Traveling with Children

For the executive combining business with vacation, traveling with family members requires a separate risk assessment. Travel is a great opportunity for children, provided the risk is minimized. Protecting children presents particular security problems when traveling, but, depending on their age, they can be taught to play a vital part in their own defense. Children who are old enough to understand should be taught all the relevant aspects of travel-safety street smarts as previously outlined. They can then play an active role in maintaining their parents' safety awareness as well as their own.

Children must be particularly warned about the dangers of talking to strangers and of wandering away from parents. They need to know at all times where safety lies, how to use a telephone, and what to do if they get lost or separated.

It's a good idea to have an emergency card in each child's possession, with at least their name, parents' names, cell-phone numbers, and hotel details.

Muslim Countries

Muslim countries deserve special mention, not only because of ongoing difficulties in the Middle East. American activity over the Palestinian question is a considerable aggravation to most Muslims. Although their hostility is usually directed at the U.S. government, it's wise not to advertise your American nationality in these countries, so leave the Stetson at home.

Muslim countries are generally very conservative in dress, though tolerance of Western garb varies from country to country. This variation is more of a problem for women, but in general, women's clothes should cover the legs and upper arms. In the more conservative Muslim societies and in the more traditional remote villages, women should also cover their heads with a shawl in public.

Be cautious in taking magazines into a Muslim country; some that seem innocuous to you may be offensive to your hosts, either for their written content or their photographs. Similarly, your private photos of your wife or daughter in a bikini may be considered an affront to public morals and confiscated by a customs officer.

Alcohol is banned in some Muslim countries but permitted in others. If you are in a country where it is banned, do not be tempted to buy or consume illicit liquor—the penalties are severe.

If you are invited into someone's home, be prepared to leave your shoes (and Western conventions) outside the door. As a general rule, eating is done with the right hand, while the left is considered unclean. Never offer to shake hands with the left hand, even if your right arm is broken. Showing the soles of the feet or shoes, or crossing your legs while seated in a chair, are also considered to be signs of disrespect.

Public displays of affection involving women are frowned on, even between married couples. Do not caress your wife or significant other in public. By contrast, you might frequently see local men holding hands; this implies nothing other than friendship.

Muslims pray several times a day at prescribed times. It is rude to talk or eat during prayers, and in some societies you will be expected to stop work during the official prayer time.

Ramadan is the Muslim holy month of prayer and daytime fasting. Your hosts will appreciate your consideration if you refrain from eating or drinking in front of them during daylight hours. You'll find that after sunset they become much more sociable.

Women play a subservient role to men in many Muslim societies, and are expected to be extremely reticent in public. Gentlemen, do not approach or attempt to strike up a conversation with a local woman. It could lead to problems for both of you.

For Western women visiting Muslim countries, modesty in dress and behavior is important. Even as a businesswoman, you will be treated with respect, but do not expect to be treated equally. You might find that men are reluctant to shake your hand, so do not offer yours first. In conservative areas, you might be expected to dine separately from the men; do not consider this an affront, but a different cultural experience.

WHEN THINGS GO WRONG

SAFETY WHEN TRAVELING is largely a matter of preparation, precautions, and vigilance. If you diligently follow the guidelines in the earlier chapters, you will considerably reduce the chances of becoming the victim of criminal assault. However, an accident or assault could happen at any time, and something unexpected might happen to you despite all precautions. This chapter deals with such unlikely events.

The first tip is to keep your emergency card with you at all times. If you are incapacitated, it will provide useful information for the emergency services. If you're separated from the rest of your belongings, the card will provide you with the contact numbers for your first line of assistance.

Contacting the Embassy or Consulate

The phone number of the embassy or consulate should be on your emergency card and programmed into your cell phone. Consular assistance, though limited by legislation, may be very useful.

The U.S. Consulate can provide lists of English-speaking doctors, dentists, and medical facilities. The consulate will assist if you lose your passport. If you lose your money, the consulate will help you get funds transferred from your home or business.

Sickness or Injury

Remember that you are more vulnerable to criminal assault when sick or injured. Treat even a minor injury or sickness more seriously than you would at home. Get medical treatment promptly, and retire to the security of your hotel until you've recovered sufficiently to move around safely.

In selecting an English-speaking doctor, seek advice from the hotel, as well as the U.S. consulate or your insurance company. Major hotels abroad usually have a good doctor available for emergency treatment of guests.

Family doctors in most countries are well trained and licensed; in Europe and some Asian countries, the hospitals and medical service are as good as in the USA. However, in some Third World countries, the latest medicines or drugs may be unavailable. A further problem is the lack of hygiene in the clinics and hospitals of many poorer countries, whereby there is risk of catching a serious disease. If in doubt, insist on using your own syringes for any needed blood tests and injections, and steer clear of the clinics if you can be treated at your hotel. If you or a member of your party is hospitalized and in need of blood in a Third World country where you suspect supplies may be contaminated, find a donor within your group or among trusted employees at your local office.

You can fly home on your commercial airline to the USA with a broken leg, even in a wheelchair, but not with an infectious disease or an injury requiring continuous medical supervision. In case of a serious injury or sickness, do not hesitate to use the air-ambulance provision in your travel insurance to get back to the USA.

BRIBERY AND CORRUPTION

In developing countries, the pay of civil servants, including policemen, can be less than twenty dollars a month. This contributes to the fact that many routinely aim to enhance their pay by seeking bribes. As a businessman, presumed to be rich and on a tight schedule, you could become a target for some minor extortion. This might be at a traffic stop for a real or imaginary traffic violation, at the scene of an accident, or at any number of places where petty bureaucrats can impede your business or movements. At a traffic stop, a policeman might point out that you can accompany him to the police station, where filling out forms might take several days; or a customs officer might suggest that you return in ten days for your baggage, while the appropriate level of duty is considered.

The practical response to this is to be polite, smile, and ask if there is some way the process can be expedited, while displaying a low-dollar-value bill along with your driver's license or whatever document you are being asked to produce. For a minor problem in a developing country, five or ten dollars might take care of it. If you consider this as a tip, such as you would give the waiter in your hotel, you won't feel too badly about it. If you argue or refuse on principle, you will at least be subjected to further delays. Handling this kind of problem should be part of the advice you seek from your local office, business acquaintances, or expatriate friends, before arriving in the country.

Paying such "gratuities" to expedite your business must not, of course, extend to the payment of bribes to secure a business contract. Such payments would violate the Foreign Corrupt Practices Act (FCPA), which could land you in a federal penitentiary for several years, along with a substantial fine, and put your company in serious trouble in the USA, apart from any immediate legal difficulties you could face in the country concerned. The Department of Justice states: "The anti-bribery provisions of the FCPA make it unlawful for a U.S. person, and certain foreign issuers of securities, to make a corrupt payment to a foreign official for the purpose of obtaining or retaining business for or with, or directing business to, any person. Since 1998, they also apply to foreign firms and persons who take any act in furtherance of such a corrupt payment while in the United States." Further details of the FCPA are available at the Department of Justice Web site link, http://www.usdoj. gov/criminal/fraud/fcpa/dojdocb.htm.

If You Get Arrested

If you are arrested overseas, the U.S. consulate staff will assist you upon request, to the degree of visiting you, advising you of your rights under local law, ensuring that you are properly treated, and providing you with a list of attorneys. They provide advice but cannot normally get you out of jail. They will notify your friends or business of your predicament and whereabouts if you wish. Insist on calling the consulate if you are arrested overseas, and meanwhile admit nothing and sign nothing. When a consular official arrives, be sure to ask for some identification and verify his credentials before discussing your predicament.

In case of arrest you might ultimately receive more practical help from your local business contacts than from the consulate, particularly in a developing country, so contact them, too. Your local business contacts will be likely to know the ropes and what it takes to get you out. In the case of a minor offense in certain developing countries, for example, it is common practice for an early release to be expedited by a third party with money and suitable connections.

Remember that in developing countries you might have fewer legal rights than in the USA. Many countries follow the Napoleonic code of justice, whereby an arrested person is guilty until proven innocent. Some Muslim countries try prisoners according to Sharia (Muslim) law. Therefore keep on the right side of the law.

It must be said that even in developing countries, the wrongful arrest of businessmen for extortion is most unusual; it is after all bound to be bad for international relations and bad for the local economy. More than 70 percent of arrests of American citizens abroad involve drug-related offenses, typically committed by tourists possessing or dealing in drugs.

ACCIDENTS WHILE DRIVING

If you get into a traffic accident abroad, keep calm. Do not get into an argument or fight over a traffic accident, as you could easily make your situation worse.

Accidents Involving Other Vehicles

Immediately assess whether there is any other danger: was the accident truly an accident, or possibly a way to stop you? Sometimes, robbers will stage an accident or jolt your car from behind. If in doubt, drive on, note the license-plate details of the other vehicle in your rearview mirror if you can call the police on your mobile phone, and stop at the next point of safety such as a police station.

If Someone is Injured or Killed

In a genuine accident where a third party is killed or injured, call the emergency services or have someone else call. Do not give your cell phone to a stranger to make the emergency services call—you might not see the stranger or your phone again. You can offer first aid to an injured person if you are qualified.

Leaving the Scene of an Accident

It is usually illegal to leave the scene of an accident if someone else is involved, and you should do so only if there is risk to yourself in staying put and waiting for the police. Unless the accident was staged as part of a kidnap or holdup, if someone is injured, the main danger might be from a hostile crowd. If such a crowd gathers, try to make your exit by driving off—possibly under the pretext of parking your vehicle.

If you elect to leave the scene of an accident because of concern for your own safety, you must stop at the nearest police station and report it. Immediately call the U.S. consulate or embassy for further advice, and alert any local colleagues or friends, giving your location and phone number.

Although it is likely to be an offense to leave the scene of an accident, it may be the lesser of two evils. This is an on-the-spot decision you have to make for yourself, and live with the consequences. In case you are obliged to leave the scene of an accident, report the incident as quickly as possible, and face the legal fallout if necessary. Do not be tempted to evade justice by failing to report an accident—it then becomes a hit-and-run case and you become a fugitive.

HOTEL FIRE

If a fire alarm sounds or there is other evidence of fire, do not panic, but move fast. Minutes count in any fire in a building. Even if you cannot see flames, smoke and poisonous fumes can build up quickly and impede your escape. If you are in your room, quickly put on some clothes and shoes. Shoes will be important if you have to walk through broken glass or hot embers, or if you have to jump. Wetted down, clothes can save you from burning and smoke inhalation. Grab a flashlight to help guide you, and possibly to signal your location. Grab your passport, money, cell phone, and car keys only if they are immediately available, and put them in your pockets. Leave everything else—you need both hands free.

If the fire alarm is ringing and your own room is not on fire, use the back of your hand to feel the door for heat before opening it. Open the door cautiously, keeping your face and body away from the opening, then check outside for smoke or flames.

Unless the corridor is on fire, make your way quickly to the nearest fire escape. If conditions are smoky, crawl—the air will be cooler and cleaner lower down. Use a shirt or wet towel to cover your face, if necessary, to help filter the smoke and gases. Get down the fire escape and outside as fast as possible.

If the fire is below you and the fire escape is blocked, go back and locate another fire escape in a different part of the building. Avoid the temptation to go up, unless you know there is another escape route there, and do not use the elevator, as you could get trapped or deposited in the middle of the fire.

If you are trapped in your room by flames or overwhelming smoke outside your door, fill the bathtub or shower with water, wet some towels or blankets, and put them around the door seals to keep smoke out. Call the hotel operator, say where you are trapped, and ask what part of the building the fire is in. Call someone outside the hotel if you have a local contact, so they can tell the emergency services where you are. Give them your cell phone number and then make sure you keep your cell phone with you. It is possible that someone outside, with a view of the hotel, can help guide you away from danger.

In extreme circumstances, consider an escape from the outside of the building. Does your room have a balcony? Could you get to the floor below? Will you need to use sheets or other improvised ropes to get down? Figure all this out and make your preparations before you open an outside door or window, as outside air may fan the fire. Even if you can't get all the way to the ground floor, you may be able to descend one level on the outside of the building, then get back in and use the fire escape from the floor below. Make sure you take something to help you break in through a window below—even a glass ashtray in your pocket.

Once you get out of the building, get well away. A burning building presents a danger from falling debris, explosions, and breaking glass, and you need to be out of the way of firefighters and rescue services.

CRIMINAL ASSAULT

Pickpockets are the most common of thieves. They frequently operate in pairs or groups, one acting as a distraction agent, possibly bumping into the target, while another rifles the victim's pockets. If a prospective pickpocket jostles you, shout to attract attention, shake him off, and move away. Do not immediately pat your pocket to check on your wallet, as this is a giveaway for another pickpocket.

Armed robbery is a more serious crime, as you can get seriously hurt. If you are held up or mugged by someone armed with a knife or gun, hand over your money or valuables immediately. Do not resist—it's not worth risking your life over a few dollars. If you have taken our advice and limited what you have in your wallet, or used a throwaway wallet, you won't have lost much, anyway. Get away from the scene of the robbery and into a safe spot immediately, before your assailant decides you should be worth more.

Banks and ATMs are favorite haunts of armed robbers because customers have usually just drawn out money. Although a bank or ATM may be monitored by security cameras, these are not always operational, frequently have blind spots, and are no deterrent to a masked robber, anyway. If while using an ATM you think you are about to be held up, press the cancel button and leave the location immediately. Abandon your money or ATM card if necessary. Be extremely vigilant when leaving an ATM or bank to ensure that you are not being followed.

If you are being attacked for your money or valuables, the best advice is to give it away, throw it down away from you to distract your attacker, then make your escape immediately.

There is no plan to suit all occasions if you are attacked, but you should try to stall or distract your attacker while planning a way to safety. It's impossible to guess an assailant's intentions, so do not believe you will be safe after giving up your possessions or your clothes.

You should avoid close-quarter fighting, as you never know who or what you're up against. However, if there is no way to escape and your life is in immediate danger, for instance you are cornered and in danger of being stabbed, you may have to fight briefly to get into a position to get away. Remember that you are not trying to win a prizefight, only to escape unharmed, while your opponent may be larger, fitter, crazy, and have similar accomplices. Use any available weapon to defend yourself: stones, a ballpoint pen, or a belt with a buckle. Face your assailant, try to circle, and use surprise and aggression to inflict some damage while seizing the first opportunity to break away and escape. Then run for safety, while yelling to attract attention.

Memorize your attacker's features and getaway vehicle if there is one. Jot down details as soon as possible, using a pencil, lipstick, blood, dirt or whatever is available. A vehicle registration number or good description of an assailant may help the police make a quick arrest.

Notify the police as soon as possible after an assault. If you lose any credit cards, airline tickets, or travel documents, immediately call the credit-card company, airline, or consular office as appropriate.

Kidnap

Considering the statistics, the likelihood of getting involved in a kidnap may seem remote to the average business traveler staying away from places like Bogotá. Indeed, if you follow the precautions recommended above, including increased personal protection if you must visit high-risk areas, the chance is considerably reduced. However, it's best to have a contingency plan so that you will have considered, however unlikely the chance of kidnap, what your course of action should be.

Remember that a kidnap may be a short-term abduction such as an express kidnap for extortion, or a longer-term situation for a negotiated ransom or political goals. Your abductors may be small-time criminals, political zealots, or religious fanatics.

Immediate Action

In an abduction attempt, scream and fight (unless a weapon is being used against you) to attract attention. Even if no one comes to your rescue, someone might note the details of the abductors and report the incident to the police.

Once you are abducted, do not waste your energy resisting, but try to stay calm and figure out your situation. The sooner you start analyzing it the better. Whether you are abducted on foot or by vehicle, memorize your route as far as possible: if you escape, you have to know how to get back; if you can make a call, you'll need to tell rescuers where you are.

You could be forced into the trunk of a car or blindfolded, but even if you can't see, make a mental note of the time traveled, estimate the direction from sun and shadows, and remember sounds and smells such as railways or factories, as well as road features such as stops, steep gradients, and sharp turns. Leave a trail or clues if possible.

If you can escape with a good chance to get clear, seize the moment, even if its means throwing yourself out of a slow-moving car. The longer you are held, the more securely you will be confined, and the more difficult it will be to escape.

Do not try to escape unless there is a good chance to get clear, as you might get only one opportunity. If you can escape from a car, pick the place: a crowded street, a nearby police car, a one-way street, wherever immediate recapture is difficult.

Confinement

If you find yourself securely held, then cooperate with your captors while still looking for a chance to escape. Find out what they hope to gain from your kidnap, whether ransom, political advantage, prisoner exchange, or other goals, so that you understand their motives.

You should cooperate with your captors if you can do so without divulging anything that could be used against you or others. Do not antagonize them, but be friendly. Establish a rapport if your kidnappers will talk, and find out about their personal lives. They may be less inclined, or hesitate, to kill you if things go wrong.

Be prepared for a long confinement and do not lose heart. Keep track of time. Keep a diary or tick off the days on a wall.

Keep track of the guards: how many there are, their routine, what weapons they have and where they keep them, who the leader is, and who is likely to be the softest.

Stay mentally alert and keep fit. You can do physical exercises in a confined place. Eat and drink as much as you can. Mental exercises can include reciting poetry, mathematical problem solving, memorizing people and places, and even learning the local language.

Group Dynamics

If you are in a group of hostages, the team dynamic will be important to your survival. Inventory your joint physical assets. Matches, penknives, mirrors, and shoelaces may all become useful as weapons or escape tools.

Inventory your group's personal assets. Who has medical training or language skills? Does anyone have military training or weapons-handling skills?

Discuss your environment to figure out where you are located. If one of you escaped or could make a call or send a message, could he quickly direct a rescue party back to the location?

Communicate as much as you can. Support each other; tell jokes and stories and sing songs if you are allowed to. Take the opportunity to establish a communication plan, in case you are split up or later not allowed to talk.

If you are sure that there is not a member of the kidnappers' organization hidden among your hostage party, prepare a group escape plan and discuss what to do if things turn nasty and your lives are at immediate risk. Consider overpowering a guard and snatching a weapon.

Escape

Continuously review opportunities and escape options. Try to escape only when there is a good chance of success, or if you are about to be killed. A failed escape attempt could lead to violence, as well as stricter confinement that makes further attempts more difficult.

Establish a signal plan to use if rescuers or police are nearby. Consider signaling with a mirror, making a loud noise, or even setting fire to your surroundings.

If you escape from custody, get to a safe place as fast as possible to avoid recapture. Depending on the local situation, this could be a secure hotel, a police station, or a U.S. or allied embassy.

Hostage Negotiations

If you are the subject of kidnap and subsequent hostage negotiations, try to keep calm. Whatever you do, avoid threatening behavior or language. You have some perceived value in the kidnappers' eyes, and most will want to trade you alive. Of course, you do not want to make yourself more valuable than they already think you are. If you happen to be caught up in a group kidnapping or hostage situation, do not volunteer the fact that you are the president of United Widgets or mayor of your hometown. In fact, if you are carrying any such identifying information, dispose of it as quickly and discretely as you can.

Be prepared for the fact that ransom negotiations following a kidnap often take a long time, sometimes months. The U.S. government does not bow to ransom demands, on the theory that doing so leads to further kidnaps. On the other hand, depending on circumstances, they might get involved in negotiations and even a rescue attempt for their own citizens. The U.S. government department concerned would normally be the FBI.

Ransom demands are usually made to a victim's family or employer. This may be the moment when you receive a candid assessment of your worth!

Ransom Demands

If you are on the receiving end of a kidnap and ransom demand, as a corporation or individual, get professional advice. Do not call the local police, or try to negotiate details yourself, or "nickel and dime" on behalf of your company. Remember that someone's life is on the line. Wise corporations have well-rehearsed contingency plans for this sort of event, handled by a designated, trained crisis response team.

The U.S. Government may play a role in handling a ransom demand for one or more of its citizens, particularly if the demand is of a political or terrorist nature. Additionally, there are various private security firms that specialize in handling international ransom negotiations. In the event of receiving a ransom demand, one of these firms should be engaged immediately to advise and assist the crisis management team. If K&R insurance coverage is in place, then the first place to seek professional help is from the insurance company. K&R insurance typically provides for a professional negotiator to fly into the country and handle negotiations.

For a corporation at the receiving end of a ransom demand, the first consideration is the safety of the employee and how to react to the demands. Beyond that, there are the needs for secrecy, for press management, for the security of other employees, for care of the victim's family, and for minimizing business impact.

WHAT TO DO IF CAUGHT IN A CROSSFIRE

Unarmed members of the public occasionally find themselves caught up in a situation where gunfire erupts around them. This could be the scene of an armed robbery, a hijack attempt, or an act of terrorism. If you are in the vicinity when shooting breaks out, your first reaction should be to drop to the ground. Identify where the shooting comes from and crawl behind the nearest solid piece of cover. Stay there until it is safe to move.

If you are in the area of a bomb blast, do not converge on the scene; there could be a second bomb. Keep down, find some cover, and stay away. Get well away from glass windows. Wait for the security services to secure the area, and only approach them if you have a reason to do so, such as to report as a witness or to search for a missing partner.

PLANE OR BUILDING HIJACK

In many building hijacks, some people manage to escape in the initial moments of confusion. They are either smart or just lucky. An airborne hijack offers no such opportunity for immediate escape, but it must be said that the chances of being present during a plane hijack are very slim. Statistically, you're more likely to die at home from a lightning strike. However, if a hijack or other onboard emergency occurs during your flight, keep calm and follow the flight crew's directions.

In its simplest form, a plane hijack or a building hostage situation may involve only one attacker. There have been several such cases where, typically, a deranged passenger attempts to storm the cockpit of a plane, a bank robbery goes wrong, or a jilted husband seizes a handful of hostages in a building. Most of these cases eventually end safely for the hostages. Often, in the case of one-man plane hijack attempts, an alert flight crew foils the try. A flight steward thwarted one attempt on an Air New Zealand flight by wielding a whisky bottle to great effect on the hijacker's head. More serious was the attempted bombing of an American Airlines flight in December 2001 by the "Shoe Bomber," who was pinned down by an alert flight attendant and fellow passengers while attempting to light the fuse in one of his shoes. Vigilance and quick action saved the day in both cases.

It's harder to foil a hijacking by an armed terrorist gang, because of the difficulty of trying to simultaneously overwhelm several armed men who are scattered around the cabin. Until September 11, 2001, most hijacks either ended in negotiation on the ground, with the eventual release of the passengers and crew, or in the successful storming of the aircraft by special forces. Most of the casualties in these cases were passengers who angered or resisted the hijackers. Routine advice in the case of hijack has been to follow instructions, avoid eye contact, keep quiet, and hold out until negotiation or rescue is effected.

Of course, if you determine that your plane has been hijacked by suicidal fanatics bent on using it as a weapon, it might be best for a few fit passengers to rush them, as in the case of one of the doomed September 11 flights. Remember, however, that there may be armed sky marshals on board waiting for an opportunity to make a move—do not get in their way.

If you are detained in a hijack situation, whether plane or building, try to assess the numbers and memorize the identity of the hijackers, but never assume that you have identified them all; one or more may still be hidden among the passengers. Make a mental note of their weapons and equipment, too, in case you get released before some of the other hostages and are able to assist the security forces in their threat assessment.

RESCUE

A plane on the ground, or a seized building, may be stormed by security forces, especially if negotiations break down and hostages are being killed. In this case, you can expect surprise, overwhelming shock, stun grenades, and shooting.

This rescue assault is the most dangerous moment, and your part in the operation is to try to stay safe. In a rescue attempt, keep down, cover your head with your arms, and breathe through a handkerchief or sweater if smoke or gas is evident. Do not stand up until you are told it is safe to do so, as a hijacker, a member of the rescue squad, or both, could shoot you. Then keep your hands in the air, and without making any sudden motions, which might be misinterpreted, move out as directed.

A plane evacuation in these circumstances may involve use of the emergency doors and escape chutes, if they are still operational. In any event, once out of the plane, move away rapidly in case there is a subsequent fuel fire or explosion.

Security forces in a hostage rescue usually assume that there are still terrorists hiding among the hostages, and treat everyone as suspect until they have had time to search and question all the former hostages. Expect to be handled forcefully until your identity has been verified.

Summary

Despite increased terrorist activity around the world, statistically, rising crime presents far more risk to travelers. Criminals look for easy pickings—defenseless, unsuspecting, rich, sitting targets—and a secure escape route. You can avoid being a target by following the steps you have read in this Manual. Careful preparation for travel, increased personal awareness, and a good grasp of precautionary measures and street smarts will invariably keep the intelligent traveler out of harm's way.

If you are a new or occasional traveler, do not be deterred by the risks of travel. Rather, use this Manual to make yourself aware of the risks and to prepare yourself to avoid them. If you are a frequent traveler, use this Manual to assess your own travel-safety practices. You will find that there are many areas you can improve on to ensure that your future journeys are safe and pleasant.

Travel is the opportunity of a lifetime, to see new horizons, to study other cultures, and to meet different people. It gives us the power to develop international relations, to establish and further international understanding, and to benefit from international commerce. Travel should be educational, profitable in many different ways, and above all, entertaining. Therefore, be safe, and enjoy the experience.

Appendix A:

Carry-on Luggage

Airline Club cards
Airline Tickets
Business cards
Camera (make it a small one) with film
Cash: local currency in small denominations
Cell phone with charger and ancillaries
Contact list and emergency card
Credit cards
Driver's license
Flashlight (small LED type)
International Driving Permit or alternative spare ID
Itinerary, with reservation or confirmation numbers and contact telephone numbers
Maps.
Passport (with visa if needed)
PDA or laptop, with charger and ancillaries
Pens
Prescription medication, in its original container, with the prescription, and doctor's note if necessary
Reading glasses if you use them
Travel insurance or medical insurance card or policy
Traveler's checks (signed)
Vaccination certificate

APPENDIX B:

Check-in Baggage

In addition to the usual clothes, shoes, sports wear and toiletries:

Company stationery
Cord for securing bags, doors, (doubles as clothesline)
Door jamb
First aid and medical kit (non-prescription items).
Insect repellent and mosquito net
Laptop locking kit
Pen knife (keep it in your check-in baggage until you arrive)
Phrase book or dictionary
Plug adapters for international electric outlets
Portable radio with short-wave band
Small roll of duct tape
Spare batteries for phone, camera, and laptop
Spare LED flashlight*
Sun hat and sun glasses
Sun screen
Unclassified (public domain) company literature

---

* (These are smaller, brighter, and longer lasting than conventional flashlights, and make nice handouts when you are leaving).

Appendix C:

Emergency Card

Make an emergency telephone contact list on a small card and keep it with you at all times.

1. Personal Data

Your name, blood type, allergies, medications used, home physician and details of an emergency contact person

2. Home List

◆ *An office emergency contact person, including home and mobile numbers (direct numbers only; remember 800 numbers do not work from overseas)*

◆ *A trusted friend or neighbor, including business, home, mobile numbers and e-mail*

◆ *Your travel/medical insurance company, with policy number Credit-card company (and your card number*)*

---

* It is a good idea to transpose a couple of digits when making a record of your credit card and calling card numbers. That way if someone else sees your record they can not fraudulently use your name and card number.

3. OVERSEAS LIST

◆ *Your Hotel, name address and phone number*

◆ *Car rental office local phone number and reservation number*

◆ *Local office or business partner*

◆ *A local home number (friend or business contact)*

◆ *U.S. embassy or consulate*

◆ *Local police and ambulance emergency numbers*

◆ *Your insurance local number*

◆ *International calling card (AT&T or other)*

Appendix D:

First Aid and Medical Kit

Discuss the list with your doctor, based on the country or countries you are visiting:

Antibiotics, such as Augmentin
Anti Malarial pills
Antiseptic dressings
Antiseptic ointment
Aspirin
Band Aids
Bandages
Disinfectant hand wipes
Eye drops
Insect repellent
Pain killers, Tylenol or similar
Respiratory face masks
Scissors; tweezers (to extract splinters)
Stomach medicine, Immodium or similar
Sunscreen
Syringes and needles
Tissue adhesive glue
Water purification tablets

Appendix E:

Duplicate Documents

You should leave copies of the following documents at your office or with a trusted friend, in case the originals get lost or stolen during your trip. If any of these documents does get lost, a copy can then quickly be faxed to you if required to facilitate replacement. Write down the direct phone numbers—not toll-free numbers, which don't work from abroad—of the issuing airlines, banks, and credit-card companies, so you know whom to call if any of your documents is lost or stolen. Be sure to include your emergency contact details, such as a close relative who should be advised in case you are incapacitated during your trip. Include your mobile phone number abroad and your e-mail address.

Airline ticket
Car rental bookings with confirmation numbers
Credit cards
Detailed Itinerary with dates, flights, inland travel, hotels, and local contacts
Drivers license
Hotel bookings with confirmation numbers
Passport
Travel and Medical Insurance details
Traveler's check serial numbers
Vaccination certificates

APPENDIX F:

Pre-travel Check List

RESEARCH AND PREPARATION

Check for Travel Advisories by calling the State Department, 202-647-5225, or on the Internet at http://travel.state.gov.

Contact the embassy of the country you are visiting to review security and hotels.

Contact business associates or social contacts in country to assess local situation.

Find out about any health threats at your destination, and vaccination requirements, by contacting the Centers for Disease Control, on the Web, http://www.cdc.gov/ or call the travelers' hot line at 1-888-232-3228.

Check your medical insurance and review the list of local doctors and hospitals.

Get visas and vaccinations organized.

Check your passport validity period.

Order foreign currency and traveler's checks.

Get a country map and a local or city map.

Make flight reservations.

Call potential hotels to conduct security check.

Select and make hotel reservations.

Arrange for international cell phone service.

Make and print your home and overseas contact lists.

Make an emergency contact card.

Check local driving regulations and signs.

Decide on local means of transportation.

Book a rental car if needed, and write down the confirmation number. Ask for an airport map and directions to the rental office desk and car park.

Or:

Arrange to be met at the destination airport. If using a hotel or company limo, arrange recognition and password or phrase.

Remove sensitive data from your laptop and back it up.

Encrypt all remaining data files on your laptop (or PDA).

Collect and sign traveler's checks.

Make two copies of your traveler's check serial-number list, one to take with you, the other to leave at home or office.

Provide an itinerary for your office and give a copy to your trusted friend.

Agree on a communications plan and emergency code words.

Weed out unnecessary credit cards and information from your wallet.

Duplicate your essential documents per Appendix E.

Arrange a ride to the departure airport.

Check the State Department's Travel Advisories one last time.

Home Security

Arrange a house sitter.

Make arrangements for care of pets.

Cancel newspapers and deliveries.

Brief the trusted neighbor.

Stow ladders and tools indoors.

Dispose of garbage.

Switch off heaters and air conditioners.

Unplug electric appliances.

Make sure all water faucets are off.

Close drapes.

Lock all doors and windows.

Lock all outbuildings and vehicles.

Put a couple of lights and a radio on timers.

Activate the alarm system.

APPENDIX G:

Useful Internet Addresses

The following addresses are provided for the reader's consideration, and as a start point for further research. They are not endorsements of any service or product.

Australian Government travel advisories
www.dfat.gov.au/consular/advice

BBC International News
www.bbbc.co.uk

Cell Phone rental
http://www.rentcell.com/

Center for Disease Control
www.cdc.gov

CIA Fact book
www.cia.gov/cia/publications/factbook/

CNN
www.cnn.com

International Travel Safety
http://www.travelsafetycorp.com/

National Transportation Safety Board
www.ntsb.gov

Overseas Road Safety
www.travel.state.gov/road_safety.html

Overseas Security Advisory Council
www.ds-osac.org

Security and Safety products
http://nservices.com/security.htm

Stratfor Strategic forecasting
www.stratfor.com

State Department
www.travel.state.gov

State Department Key Officers in Foreign Posts
http://foia.state.gov/MMS/KOH/keyofficers.asp

Travel Advisories
www.travel.state.gov/travel_warnings.html

Travel Health Online
www.tripprep.com

UK Government travel advisories
www.fco.gov.uk/travel

US Embassies overseas
http://usembassy.state.gov/

Weather Worldwide
www.weather.com

World Health Organization
www.who.int/en/

Voice of America News
http://www.voanews.com/

World Trade Organization
http://www.wto.org/

World travel net
http://www.world-travel-net.com/

XE.com Currency convertor
http://www.xe.com/

TALLY HO
CONSULTING

Quick Order Form

Fax Orders: **415.662.2287. Fill out and fax this form.**
Internet Orders: **www.TallyHoConsulting.com**
E-mail Orders: **orders@TallyHoConsulting.com**
Postal Orders: **Tally Ho Consulting,**
PO Box 127 • Nicasio • CA 94946

The Personal Travel Safety Manual
by Christopher P. P. Barnes

✐ **No. of books ordered @ $18.95 each**		Subtotal ☞	
Shipping by Air **US addresses:** $4.00 for first book and $2.00 for each accompanying additional book. **International:** $9.00 for first book and $5.00 for each accompanying additional book.		7.75% sales tax (CA residents only)	
		Shipping & handling	
		Total	

Name

Address

City

State   Zip

○ Check enclosed
Charge to: ○ VISA   ○ MasterCard   ○ Discover   ○ American Express

Card Number	Expiration Date

Authorized Signature	Daytime Phone Number

E-mail